Michael Jordan

by David Pietrusza

Lucent Books, San Diego, CA

Titles in the People in the News series include:
Bill Gates
Michael Jordan
Dominique Moceanu
The Rolling Stones
Steven Spielberg
Oprah Winfrey

Library of Congress Cataloging-in-Publication Data

Pietrusza, David, 1949–
  Michael Jordan / by David Pietrusza.
    p. cm. — (People in the news)
  Includes bibliographical references (p.   ) and index.
  ISBN 1-56006-350-5 (lib. : alk. paper)
  1. Jordan, Michael, 1963–   . 2. Basketball players—United
States—Biography. 3. Chicago Bulls (Basketball team)
  I. Title. II. Series: People in the news (San Diego, Calif.)
GV884.J67P54   1999
796.323'092—dc21
[B]   98-22485
                                                                  CIP

Copyright © 1999 by Lucent Books, Inc.
P.O. Box 289011
San Diego, CA 92198-9011
Printed in the U.S.A.

Table of Contents

69899

Foreword

FAME AND CELEBRITY are alluring. People are drawn to those who walk in fame's spotlight, whether they are known for great accomplishments or for notorious deeds. The lives of the famous pique public interest and attract attention, perhaps because their experiences seem in some ways so different from, yet in other ways so similar to, our own.

Newspapers, magazines, and television regularly capitalize on this fascination with celebrity by running profiles of famous people. For example, television programs such as *Entertainment Tonight* devote all of their programming to stories about entertainment and entertainers. Magazines such as *People* fill their pages with stories of the private lives of famous people. Even newspapers, newsmagazines, and television news frequently delve into the lives of well-known personalities. Despite the number of articles and programs, few provide more than a superficial glimpse at their subjects.

Lucent's People in the News series offers young readers a deeper look into the lives of today's newsmakers, the influences that have shaped them, and the impact they have had in their fields of endeavor and on other people's lives. The subjects of the series hail from many disciplines and walks of life. They include authors, musicians, athletes, political leaders, entertainers, entrepreneurs, and others who have made a mark on modern life and who, in many cases, will continue to do so for years to come.

These biographies are more than factual chronicles. Each book emphasizes the contributions, accomplishments, or deeds that have brought fame or notoriety to the individual and shows how that person has influenced modern life. Authors portray their subjects in a realistic, unsentimental light. For example, Bill Gates—the cofounder and chief executive officer of the software giant Microsoft—has been instrumental in making personal computers the most vital tool of the modern age. Few dispute his business savvy, his perseverance, or his technical expertise, yet critics say he is ruthless in his dealings with competitors and driven more by his desire to maintain Microsoft's dominance in the computer industry than by an interest in furthering technology.

In these books, young readers will encounter inspiring stories about real people who achieved success despite enormous obstacles. Oprah Winfrey—the most powerful, most watched, and wealthiest woman on television today—spent the first six years of her life in the care of her grandparents while her unwed mother sought work and a better life elsewhere. Her adolescence was colored by promiscuity, pregnancy at age fourteen, rape, and sexual abuse.

Each author documents and supports his or her work with an array of primary and secondary source quotations taken from diaries, letters, speeches, and interviews. All quotes are footnoted to show readers exactly how and where biographers derive their information and provide guidance for further research. The quotations enliven the text by giving readers eyewitness views of the life and accomplishments of each person covered in the People in the News series.

In addition, each book in the series includes photographs, annotated bibliographies, timelines, and comprehensive indexes. For both the casual reader and the student researcher, the People in the News series offers insight into the lives of today's newsmakers—people who shape the way we live, work, and play in the modern age.

Introduction

His Air-ness

EVERY ERA BOASTS its share of great athletes. But only a few of them are able to achieve true superstardom and move from being merely well-known and beloved within the sports world to being idolized by a far wider audience—to becoming cultural icons.

National Basketball Association (NBA) star Michael Jordan is one such athlete. It is no exaggeration to say that the high-scoring Chicago Bulls guard may be the most popular athlete since Babe Ruth transformed the game of baseball in the 1920s from a hit-and-run sport into a power game. Many great athletes have performed since Ruth retired—Jackie Robinson, Mickey Mantle, Joe Namath, Muhammad Ali, Wilt Chamberlain, Billy Jean King, Joe Montana, and Wayne Gretzky, to name just a few—but Jordan has come closest to duplicating what the Babe accomplished: combining tremendous, almost-superhuman, playing achievements with a personality that lights up any room and makes him almost universally beloved.

"I used to think that Michael Jordan was the Babe Ruth of basketball," Bulls owner Jerry Reinsdorf once said, "I have now come to believe that Babe Ruth was the Michael Jordan of baseball."[1]

Before Jordan, some basketball superstars—such as Wilt Chamberlain—had specialized in scoring; others—such as Bill Russell—had excelled on defense. Jordan consistently led the league in scoring. He seemed to soar through the air—and remain there—maintaining a "hang time" no other player had. He could pass, drive, rebound, defend, ballhandle. He could do it all. "What would be Jordan's greatest personal accomplishment," noted sportswriter Jack McCallum, "was evident from the earliest moments of his career: He was *better* than his hype."[2]

That is a tremendous achievement. And it makes for some very profitable possibilities. Athletes have often endorsed commercial products, often with rather mediocre results. But Jordan—from the moment that he joined the NBA—raised the standard for high-profile, highly lucrative personal endorsements. In 1984 as an NBA rookie he endorsed

Michael Jordan's playing ability and personality have earned him the respect and admiration of millions of basketball fans.

Nike's Air Jordan shoes for an unprecedented fee of $2.5 million. Despite the expense, the move paid off handsomely for Nike. The company sold $130 million worth of Air Jordans in just the first two years of the contract. Later Jordan moved on to other successful personal advertising campaigns—for such companies and products as Coca-Cola, McDonald's, Gatorade, Hanes, Ball Park Franks, and Wheaties (he was the first basketball player ever to appear on a box of Wheaties). In just one two-year period (1996–97) Jordan earned an estimated $80 million in income—aside from the record $36 million Bulls salary he drew for the 1997–98 season. The combination of his tremendous talent and pleasing personality had made this possible. "Michael Jordan is the quintessential spokesperson,"[3] says Patti Sinopoli, group manager of communications and public relations for Gatorade.

Jordan's commercial success—and personal popularity—are even more important because of his race. Jordan is black, and before his arrival on the American sports scene, many African-American superstars did not receive the lucrative endorsement contracts that white athletes did. But Jordan changed all that. He proved that white fans—and consumers—

could react positively to a black superstar. Jordan's success opened the doors for other black athletes. Now others could obtain their share of endorsements and public acclaim—a share finally equivalent to their athletic achievements. Black superstars such as Bill Russell, Henry Aaron, and Willie Mays had never enjoyed such lucrative endorsement contracts despite dominating their sports. Now that would change. Michael Jordan opened the doors for the Tiger Woodses, the Ken Griffey Jrs., and even the Dennis Rodmans.

Jordan, of course, has also been tremendously popular with African-Americans. His friendliness, generosity, and community service serve as an excellent role model to young black Americans. "With the exception of [fellow NBA star] Julius Erving," observed author Nelson George in *Elevating the Game: Black Men and Basketball,* "no previous Black ball star has had the same balance of tremendous talent, poise in public, and personal charisma."[4]

Some have even said that it is no coincidence the NBA has become so hugely popular since Jordan's arrival. As recently as the late 1970s pro basketball was a threadbare proposition with limited national TV coverage. When Jordan arrived in the early 1980s, the NBA skyrocketed in popularity. Just five years after his debut, pro basketball's gross revenues nearly doubled to $300 million. In that same time, the NBA's average per-game attendance increased by nearly 4,000, to an average of 13,420. Of course, other great stars such as Magic Johnson, Larry Bird, and Charles Barkley also were coming into their own, but Jordan

Jordan's phenomenal athletic feats are partly responsible for the tremendous popularity of basketball today.

was in a class by himself. Certainly no one can deny the positive effect he had on the popularity of the Chicago Bulls. Home attendance for the Bulls soared from 6,365 per game in 1983–84 (the season before Jordan signed with them) to 11,887 in his first season with the franchise. Bulls home attendance is now over 23,000 per game.

Despite Jordan's amazing success, both on the court and in the business world, his life has not been without difficulties. Commentators—and some of his teammates—have swiped at his style of play. In the early 1990s the NBA investigated questions of Jordan's gambling and the high-stakes gamblers he was associating with. He also had to overcome a huge personal tragedy. Unlike Babe Ruth, Jordan came from a happy home. He was especially close to his father, James Jordan. When his father was senselessly murdered in July 1993, Michael was crushed. He stunned the sports world by walking away from the NBA while still at the top of his game. Then he sent out further shock waves when he tried his hand at baseball, attempting to fulfill his father's dream. In 1995 Jordan returned to the Bulls. His critics sneered that Jordan would be unable to regain his old form. Once again he proved them wrong and eventually led Chicago to three more NBA titles—for a total of six in eight years.

But despite the tragedy and the celebrity, Michael Jordan remains simply one of the very best basketball players in history. For years Jordan's critics admitted that he was a great player, but that he was not a great *team* player. As tremendous a star as Jordan was, he could not lead the Bulls to an NBA title. His Air-ness made those critics eat their words. He has led the Bulls to six championships, including the very rare feat of two "three-peats"—three titles ·in a row. When he retired in 1993, Michael Jordan thought he had nothing left to prove in basketball. After he returned—and brought the Bulls three more titles—no one could consider that idea.

Chapter 1

Growing Up in North Carolina

NOBODY IS BORN to be a superstar. Babe Ruth wasn't. Wayne Gretzky wasn't. Ken Griffey Jr. wasn't. And certainly Michael Jordan wasn't. In fact, Michael Jordan almost didn't make it past his birth. His mother's pregnancy was difficult, and not made easier by her own mother's death midway through it. A week before Michael was born, the family doctor ordered Deloris Jordan to remain in bed. He feared a miscarriage. That miscarriage nearly happened. Michael Jordan came into this world with nosebleeds and had to stay in the hospital three days after his mother left for home. The family was worried that its new son might not long survive his birth.

"My Parents Warned Me About the Traps"

Michael did survive (though he nearly electrocuted himself at age two), but the world he entered was full of very real disadvantages. The Jordan family was black and poor. Both James and Deloris Jordan came from rural sharecropping families. James Jordan was a mechanic at General Electric but he never earned a lot of money, and in addition to Michael he had four other children to support.

But Michael also had a great advantage. The Jordan family was a strong one—and a loving one. James Jordan had moved his family back from Brooklyn (where Michael was born) to North Carolina, where he thought his children would have a better chance of growing up safe and sound. James even built a small brick house for his family. He had to work nights and weekends to do it, but he did. And both parents worked to instill a firm sense of right and wrong in their children. "My parents warned me about the traps," Michael once said. "The drugs and drink, the streets that could catch you if you got careless."[5]

Michael himself was a mixed bag. He was cheerful, but he had a number of bad habits. He was not the most motivated child in the world—or even in his family. He often didn't apply himself to his studies, and when the Jordan family had chores, Michael had to be prodded over and over again to pitch in.

But as unmotivated as young Michael could be at work or studies, he was incredibly competitive at sports. His first love, however, was not basketball. It was baseball. Michael pitched and played shortstop and the outfield in Little League. He was good. As a pitcher he recorded two no-hitters.

Then Michael discovered basketball, and day after day he would compete in his backyard against his older brother, Larry. Being older, Larry beat Michael time after time. Still Michael wouldn't give up. He kept playing—and he kept working. He was determined to beat his older brother—and eventually anyone who dared take the court against him. "It's an instinct that makes me love to win and hate to lose at any game," he once remarked. "My older brother Larry used to beat me in one-on-one basketball games. He'd say something about it and I'd get ticked off and fight him."[6]

Despite the occasional childhood spats between Michael and Larry, Michael had a great deal of respect for his older

Deloris Jordan raised her children with high morals and warned them against the pitfalls of drugs and alcohol.

brother—both as a person, and as a player. Michael modeled himself after Larry. Even though Larry was just five feet, six inches tall, he could soar through the air—and he could dunk the ball. "When you see me play," Michael says, "you see Larry play."[7]

"I Closed the Door and I Cried"

But as Michael entered his teenage years he was nothing special as an athlete. True he was a decent baseball player, ran on the track team, quarterbacked the junior varsity football team and played guard on the basketball team. However, he had one very big—or rather small—problem. Just as all the Jordans, Michael was short. James and Larry Jordan were just five feet, six inches tall. Michael was only five feet, five inches tall. Then, as he entered high school Michael began to shoot up in height—growing quickly to five feet, ten inches, and eventually (when he was in college) to his full height of six feet, six inches.

Michael Jordan now had the jumping skills of brother Larry plus his own height. In his sophomore year he went out for the Laney High School varsity basketball team. He still didn't make it. Michael was shocked. He was a decent player, and he knew he was at least as good (actually better) than one competitor who had made the team.

When coach Clifton "Pop" Herring gave Jordan the news, Michael couldn't believe it. He wanted to quit basketball. He wanted to just go and hide. "I went to my room and I closed the door and I cried," Jordan once recalled. "For a while I couldn't stop."[8]

But once Michael got over the shock, he only became more resolved to be a better player. He was determined to make the varsity team and to prove Coach Herring wrong.

Actually, Herring wasn't wrong at all. He knew that Michael was better than the last player he had picked for the varsity team. But he also knew that if Michael had made the varsity team, he would have received little playing time—and it's tough to improve your game sitting on the bench. He wanted Michael to play—and to get better—and the place for that was on the junior varsity team.

"That Got Me Going Again"

Disappointment caused Michael Jordan to work harder than ever. Some people realize they have to work harder to reach their goals. Michael Jordan is such a person. When he was cut from his high school basketball team, he didn't give up. He just went back to work and kept trying. In Greg Garber's book *Hoops!* Jordan is quoted regarding how he reacted to failure:

> Being cut definitely had a big effect on me. It was embarrassing, not making the team. They posted the roster in the locker room, and it was there for a long, long time without my name on it. I remember being really mad, too, because there was a guy who made it that really wasn't as good as me. I was down about not making it for a while, and I thought about not playing anymore. Of course, I did keep playing, and whenever I was working out and got tired and figured I ought to stop, I'd close my eyes and see that list in the locker room without my name on it. That got me going again.

Michael played his heart out on the JV. He scored 28 points per game as the team's point guard. As the season was winding down, the varsity team was headed toward the state tournament. Michael—clearly the best player on the JV—hoped he would be added to the varsity roster. Again, he was disappointed. Coach Herring picked another JV player, Larry Smith, for the varsity. Herring needed rebounding in the upcoming tourney, not playmaking and scoring. The six feet, five-inch Smith was the player for the job.

Still, Jordan was determined to make the varsity team any way he could. It was nearly an obsession. Michael volunteered to be team manager. That sounded good, but all it meant was that he lugged the team equipment from gym to gym. The closest he got to any game was on the Laney bench.

The experience galled Jordan. He vowed it would never happen again. He spent the summer playing basketball, honing his skills, shooting baskets and making plays. When his next chance came he would be *ready*.

"I Set a Goal to Excel"

He would also be taller. Michael got his second growth spurt. He was no longer five feet, ten inches tall. He was six feet, 3 inches tall—and finally made the varsity. "I think Michael just willed himself to grow,"[9] said his father.

He had not yet willed himself to be a good varsity player, however. During the regular season he was clearly inconsistent. He even stood a chance of losing his job as the varsity team's point guard. Then Laney entered a holiday tournament and played against its arch rival, New Hanover. The two teams slugged it out, and it was anybody's ballgame until the fourth quarter. Then it was Michael Jordan's ballgame. He did it, rebounding, driving, passing, shooting. But with just a few seconds left, Laney High still trailed by a single point. Michael got the pass. New Hanover expected him to drive to the basket, and he started toward the hoop. But at fifteen feet out he put on the brakes and shot. The ball sailed into the basket. Laney had won— and Michael Jordan had been the star.

Jordan continued to play well that year, but Coach Herring thought he needed something more to challenge him. He recommended that Michael attend the prestigious Five Star summer basketball camp up north in Pennsylvania. Michael went—even though he wasn't sure he belonged—and dominated the three-week session. He won five trophies in his first week and was the sensation of the camp. By the end of the session Jordan had established himself as someone to watch in national basketball circles. He had grown even more and was now nearly six feet, five inches tall.

But in Michael's senior year, he ran into trouble. He began cutting classes and ignoring his studies. Laney's principal called James Jordan to tell him about the situation. James was disappointed. He told Michael that athletics were fine

James Jordan was proud of his son's playing skills, but he also emphasized the importance of education.

but that he had to knuckle down and concern himself with his education. He was jeopardizing his chance at college—and at being a college athlete. "I knew he was right and I had to change," Jordan once admitted. "I concentrated more on my schoolwork because I set a goal to excel in the classroom to reach college and I had to work to reach it."[10]

Michael had hoped to become a part of the Wolfpack of North Carolina State, but after visiting several colleges, he decided to attend the University of North Carolina (UNC). UNC had many advantages. It had a beautiful campus. Its team often found itself a place in the National Collegiate Athletic Association (NCAA) tournament. Several of its players (the Tar Heels) had gone on to the National Basketball Association (NBA), and Tar Heels coach, Dean Smith, was well respected, both as a coach and as an individual.

Jordan picked UNC before starting his senior year in high school. Freed from the distraction of the choice, he went on to score 27.8 points per game and average 12 rebounds per contest.

"The Shot"

At first Michael was nervous about being at UNC. Classes were difficult, and the competition on the court was tougher than anything he had ever before faced. But soon Michael had settled into Dean Smith's system—one that emphasized teamwork rather than the work of any one star. Jordan's teammates were quickly impressed with his skills and his attitude. He fit in right away. "I like Jordan's overall game," said teammate Jimmy Black. "He's a competitor and a hustler and we need him on the floor."[11]

In Jordan's first college game, he went 5-for-10 from the field. "I felt real comfortable out there," said Jordan. "I felt good on my shots. I did throw a bad pass, though, and I need to help out more on defense."[12]

Of course, Michael had some help on the court. Two of his teammates were future NBA stars—James Worthy and Sam Perkins. The Tar Heels finished with twenty-four victories and only two losses (24-2). Polls ranked them as the nation's number one college team.

While playing with the North Carolina Tar Heels, Jordan sharpened his athletic skills and learned the value of team play.

They were the favorites as they entered the 1982 NCAA tournament, but they barely squeaked by each game to reach the finals. There they faced a powerful Georgetown team, led by seven-foot freshman Patrick Ewing.

Before 61,612 screaming fans at New Orleans' Superdome, the Tar Heels and the Hoyas battled back and forth. In the fourth quarter, with less than a minute on the clock, Georgetown had pulled into a 62-61 lead. They expected either Worthy or Perkins to take UNC's crucial last shot. Coach Smith anticipated Georgetown's thoughts, however, and had another plan. He wanted Michael Jordan to take that shot. The Hoyas wouldn't expect that. They wouldn't expect Coach Smith to trust a freshman with the most important shot of the entire season.

But they were wrong. UNC point guard Jimmy Black threw the ball in from out of bounds to Jordan, who had moved from the right to the left side of the court to take the pass. Michael launched a sixteen-foot jump shot. Swish. UNC led 63-62, and the lead would stand up. The Tar Heels were national champions—and freshman Michael Jordan had made it happen in the first one-point NCAA Finals decision since 1959.

College Basketball Player of the Year

"The Shot" made Jordan a celebrity, nationally to some extent, but to a very large degree in North Carolina. People asked for his autograph. The local telephone directory featured a picture of "The

Shot" on its cover. A nearby restaurant named a sandwich after Michael—crab salad on pita with lettuce and tomato. "I've got a lot more friends now than I used to have," Jordan remarked. "People come up to me now and say they knew me when I was small. I don't know them, but they seem to know me."[13]

After his freshman season, Jordan went to Europe to play on a team of college All-Stars against a team of foreign basketball players. The competition was tough. And things would be tougher back at North Carolina. Michael was doing well in his studies (he maintained a B average), but the Tar Heels were seriously weakened by the loss of James Worthy, who had turned pro after his junior year. There would be even more pressure on Michael, now that Worthy, the team's leading scorer, was no longer there.

Jordan seemed to enjoy the challenge. He worked as hard as any college player ever did to increase his skills, playing for hours on end. One skill he worked on was his defense. Though he had shown flashes of offensive brilliance as a freshman, he knew that Coach Smith valued individuals who were all-around players. In Jordan's sophomore year he blossomed as a defensive star.

"I Never See You for the Color"

Michael Jordan is black, but most of his fans are not. They look up to him as a hero because of his tremendous skills and his winning personality. They look beyond the fact that he is black and they are not. One reason Jordan may be able to break through racial barriers as a public figure is because he has broken through them as an individual. In an April 15, 1990, *Chicago Tribune* article, he revealed he learned this attitude from his family:

> That's the greatest lesson I've learned from my parents. I never see you for the color. I see you for the person you are. I know I'm recognized as being black, but I don't look at you as black or white, just as a person. I think one of the reasons I've been accepted by people of so many different races is that my personality fits that. I grew up with David Bridges, who is white, since we were 5 years old, and we're still very close. I roomed with Buzz Peterson [who is white] in college.

A Foundation to Work From

Because of his well-rounded style of play Michael Jordan has been called "a one-man team." In Michael's book *I Can't Stop Trying* he gave legendary North Carolina coach Dean Smith credit for helping develop the strong fundamentals that made him great:

> "When I was at North Carolina, everybody said Dean Smith held me back. They joked about how Coach Smith was the only guy who could hold Michael Jordan under 20 points. But he taught me the game. He taught me the importance of fundamentals and how to apply them to my individual skills. That's what made me a complete player. When I got to the NBA and I had to work on different parts of my game, whether it was shooting or defense, I had that foundation to work from. I knew the way to go about it."

North Carolina coach Dean Smith helped curb Jordan's desire to show off his talent. Smith emphasized learning the basics of the game, and he instilled the belief that winning comes through teamwork.

Smith had a habit of naming a Defensive Player of the Week. In his freshman year, Jordan never won the honor. In his sophomore year he captured it twelve times. That year he averaged 20.0 points per game and was named College Basketball Player of the Year by the *Sporting News*. But the season left Michael unsatisfied. In the NCAA tourney, even though Michael led both teams in scoring with 26 points, the Tar Heels lost to the underdog Georgia Bulldogs 82-77 in the regional final. Michael didn't like to lose.

However, he didn't have to wait until his junior year to resume his winning ways. That summer he joined an all-star team that competed in the Pan-American Games, held that year in Caracas, Venezuela. His team captured the Pan-Am gold medal.

Michael's junior year saw him undergo many changes. His trips abroad interested him in geography and he became a geography major. It was also in his junior year that he first shaved his head. But Jordan began the season in a severe slump; he couldn't do anything right.

In the first half of a nationally televised game against Louisiana State University, Jordan continued to struggle. He had just three baskets in the first half. But in the second half he caught fire, leading the Tar Heels to a 90-79 victory. Jordan's season had turned around. He finished with 19.6 points per game (ppg), a 55.1 field goal average, and a 77.9 free throw average, and once

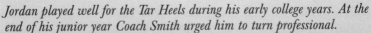

Jordan played well for the Tar Heels during his early college years. At the end of his junior year Coach Smith urged him to turn professional.

again he helped lead UNC to the NCAA tournament. For the second time, the *Sporting News* named him College Basketball Player of the Year.

Bigger Dreams, Bigger Goals

Jordan now had to prepare for his senior year—or rather he would have to decide whether he would *have* a senior year. If he wanted to, he could declare himself eligible for the NBA draft. It was not an easy decision. Michael felt he should be loyal to his school and to Coach Smith. But he also had to be realistic. If he played another year at the college level and suffered a serious injury his value to NBA teams would drop to almost nothing. Jordan wanted to be able to provide for his family.

Dean Smith helped make Jordan's decision easier. Smith had always promoted an unselfish style of play. Now, he unselfishly urged Michael to turn pro. He thought his star player was ready for the NBA. Michael Jordan announced his decision to skip his senior year at UNC and to turn pro. He was ready for a higher challenge. "I had achieved everything possible on the college level," he later revealed, "and it was time for me to go and move on to bigger dreams and bigger goals, because I had achieved everything possible." [14]

But before he would challenge the NBA, he would challenge the world.

Chapter 2

A One-Man Team

JORDAN WAS NOW playing a very high stakes game. The NBA draft could pay off for him with a multimillion dollar signing bonus and salary—or he could be bypassed in the early selections and his price would go down. In any case, he didn't want to be drafted any lower than fifth.

Michael wasn't the only highly talented player available in the 1984 draft. NBA teams had their eye on a number of top-flight college players, including Houston center Akeem Olajuwon, Kentucky center Sam Bowie, North Carolina forward-center Sam Perkins, and Auburn forward Charles Barkley.

The Houston Rockets had the first pick. They passed over Jordan and selected a player right out of their own backyard, seven-foot, one-inch center Akeem Olajuwon. The Portland Trailblazers picked next. They selected another seven-foot, one-inch center, Sam Bowie.

Now it was the Chicago Bulls' turn and they selected Jordan. Bulls general manager Jerry Krause had actually wanted to draft Bowie, but since that was no longer possible he was forced to take his next choice, Michael Jordan. On the other hand, the Bulls were not exactly Jordan's first choice—or even his second. He had wanted to be selected by the Philadelphia 76ers, a perennial playoff presence. There was no reason whatsoever for Michael to want to play with the Bulls. Chicago was among the NBA's least distinguished franchises. It had joined the league in 1966 and had not enjoyed a winning record until the club's fifth season. In 1983–84 the Bulls were just 27-55 and failed to qualify for the NBA Playoffs. Their home attendance was a mere 6,365 fans per game.

Michael had a habit of being on winning teams, but he indicated he had no problem with joining this woeful franchise. On being drafted by the Bulls, Jordan said,

> No, I've never been on a losing team before, but that doesn't bother me. You don't join any team expecting to go out there and lose. Chicago is a young team, and we have a lot of hard work ahead. The only way for the Bulls to go is up, and I'm really looking forward to making a contribution.[15]

Show Me the Money

Now, it came time to negotiate a contract between Jordan and the Bulls. He would not come cheap. Jordan knew what other top prospects were getting—and he knew he was good. The Bulls gave Jordan a seven-season $6 million contract. He would start at $550,000 in his rookie season and move up to $1 million in his fifth season. (Actually only $3.75 million and the first five years of the contract were guaranteed; the Bulls had options for $1.1 million and $1.2 million on the sixth and seventh seasons). The $6 million Jordan would receive would be the third highest amount ever paid to an NBA rookie—only Houston's Akeem Olajuwon (six years at $6.3 million plus performance bonuses) and Ralph Sampson (four years at $6.3 plus an interest-free $1 million loan back in 1983) had received more.

In his first season playing for the Chicago Bulls, Jordan earned the third highest salary ever paid to a rookie up until that time.

"No One Can Cross Those Lines"

As soon as Michael Jordan joined the NBA he faced relentless pressure from reporters peppering him with questions about what he had done—or hadn't done—on the court or off and from fans and curiosity-seekers wanting an autograph. There was, however, one place where Jordan could escape from all the tension: the basketball court. He once told author Bob Greene (who quoted him in *Rebound: The Odyssey of Michael Jordan*) how he felt:

> The basketball court for me, during a game, is the most peaceful place I can imagine. I truly feel less pressure there than anyplace I go. On the basketball court, I worry about nothing. When I'm out there, no one can bother me. Being out there is one of the most private parts of my life. . . .
>
> If my wife and I have had a disagreement at home, I know that if we have a game that night, I'll be out there on the court by myself for a few hours, and by the time I get home again at the end of the evening, all of that will have passed.
>
> The basketball court is the one place where the rules say no one can talk to me or walk up to me when I'm playing. During the game, for one of the few times in my life, I feel like I'm untouchable anywhere else. . . . Sometimes, even in the middle of a game, I'm able to think about things. As loud as it is, it's almost a quiet time for me. I know that basketball games can be very exciting, but for me the game is one of the calmest parts of my life. No one can come onto the court. No one can cross those lines. It's a very calm place.

The team was willing to pay so much because they had confidence in Michael. They were looking ahead and were afraid of how much they would have to pay once his original contract expired. They knew he was good—and they believed he would only get better.

And even more money was soon coming Jordan's way. Jordan already had someone representing him in contract negotiations and business deals, a company named ProServe (which represented such high profile athletes as tennis stars Arthur Ashe and Stan Smith). ProServe vice president David Falk arranged an endorsement contract with the Nike athletic equipment company for a new line of sneakers to be called Air Jordan. Jordan, who had yet to play a single game in the NBA, would receive $2.5 million for lending his name to the product.

But this would just be the beginning of Michael Jordan's fabulous advertising career. He would become a "natural," a successful, well-spoken, pleasant spokesperson for any number of companies and products. "There is also an undefinable quality about him," David Falk once remarked, "that if I could identify, I would bottle and sell." [16]

Going for the Gold

Before Michael Jordan could earn any of his multimillion-dollar Bulls salary, he would take a basketball detour—to Los Angeles and the 1984 Summer Olympics.

Jordan joined a number of college stars—Georgetown's Patrick Ewing, St. John's Chris Mullin, and former UNC teammate Sam Perkins—on Coach Bobby Knight's United States Olympic squad. The opportunity to play on any Olympic team is always special, but this one was particularly exciting. To tune up for Olympic competition, the U.S. team scheduled eight exhibition games against an NBA All-Star team, a team that included such greats as Larry Bird, Magic Johnson, Isiah Thomas, and Kevin McHale. Michael would soon know what it was like to face the pros—and the pros were not about to go easy on these young upstarts. Before one game, Jordan was chasing down the Olympians' practice ball. It rolled over toward Celtics star Larry Bird. Bird picked it up, but instead of flipping it to Jordan, he sneered and then drop-kicked it back over Jordan's head. "Bird was showing me it was all business now, and I was beneath him," Jordan once recalled. "I didn't forget." [17]

Bird wouldn't forget what happened next. The Olympians won eight straight games, including a bruising final game that saw them win by a lopsided 94-78 margin.

At Los Angeles, the U.S. team rolled passed China, Canada, and Uruguay to reach the finals. There they faced a tough Spanish team led by six-foot, one and one-half-inch center Fernand Romay. Michael (the team's co-captain) poured in a team-high 20 points as the U.S. crushed Spain 96-65. During the Olympics, he led Team USA with 17.1 points per game. At the ceremonies that followed the USA's final victory over Spain,

While training for the 1984 Summer Olympics, Jordan and his teammates practiced against a team of NBA All-Stars (at left). After defeating the pros, Jordan and Team USA played at the Olympics (above), earning gold medals.

Michael took his gold medal and hung it around the neck of his proud mother. Tears streamed down his cheeks.

But Jordan had done more in the Olympics than win a gold medal. He also improved his personal game. In college he had a reputation as being only able to score on drives to the basket. That's one reason he had to wait until the third round of the NBA draft. His critics said he couldn't go to the left with the ball or consistently make outside shots. With the Olympic team, Jordan worked hard to improve both skills, and he succeeded. "I improved my overall game," he later revealed, "including my outside shooting, because Coach Knight helped me to concentrate and do things without a lot of lollygagging around. So I knew I was taking everybody by surprise, including myself, when that first NBA season began." [18]

Mr. Jordan Goes to Chicago

October 26, 1984, was a historic date in NBA history. On that night Michael Jordan stepped onto the hardwood for his first game with Chicago. The scene was Chicago Stadium, home court of the Bulls; the opponents were the Washington Bullets. At first glance, it looked like Jordan did nothing special in the game. He shot 5-for-16 from the field, scoring just 16 points—only the third best on the team, behind Orlando Woolridge's 28 and Quintin Dailey's 25. But the 13,913 fans who saw the game knew differently. Jordan had seven assists and created an air of excitement in the usually quiet Chicago Stadium.

Bulls coach Kevin Loughery acknowledged Jordan may have been a little jittery in his debut but nonetheless had a lot of praise for his expensive new player: "He still did the little things for us. The steals, tipped passes, clogging up the middle, passing off to his teammates. I think Michael's presence helped the whole club. Let's face it: We won't have had the crowd and the media coverage if not for Michael Jordan." [19]

And—as they would so many times—his points *counted*. The Bulls had led for most of the game, but in the third quarter the Bullets battled back, and as the horn sounded they led 78-74. But after three Dailey baskets and two Jordan free throws, the Bulls took the lead again—and kept it.

Jordan's rookie season saw him make believers out of even the most skeptical fans. He averaged 28.2 points, 5.9 assists, and 6.5 rebounds per game. His performance won him NBA Rookie of the Year honors over Houston's Akeem Olajuwon, who had been the NBA's number one choice in the last NBA draft. The vote wasn't close. He defeated Olajuwon 57.5 to 20.5. Jordan took the honor with characteristic modesty. He commented, "I'm happy to come in and do a lot better than most people expected. It's all been a lot of fun and I've gotten a lot of enjoyment. Maybe I'll never have another season like this with all the hype and all the attention on my career." [20]

In June 1985 Michael Jordan received the Rookie of the Year award for his first season with the Bulls.

Jordan was clearly mistaken. His great rookie season was just the beginning of an even more remarkable career. In his third season he led the NBA in scoring with 37.1 ppg. In his fourth year he again led the league in scoring, really breaking through, winning every major regular season award, including Most Valuable Player, Defensive Player of the Year, All-Star Game MVP, and Slam Dunk Champion.

And, of course, it was not just a question of numbers and trophies. There was something about *how* Jordan played basketball. The amazing "hang time"—how he seemed to suspend himself in midair as he drove toward the basket. How his tongue flapped out as he slammed the ball into the hoop. How despite his relative lack of height he seemed able to do it all. Basketball had seen some great stars, but the game had *never* seen anything like Michael Jordan.

Gate Attraction

From his very beginning in the NBA, Jordan was a presence in
the league. In his first season with the Bulls, Chicago's home
attendance doubled. On television, three hundred thousand
more households were watching Bulls telecasts than before he
had joined the franchise. By his third season in the league, Bulls
games accounted for one-third of the total NBA increase in
attendance. NBA gross revenues doubled from $150 million to
$300 million in Jordan's first five years in the league. The NBA's
new popularity was no coincidence. Before his arrival the
league had been in trouble. Attendance, TV ratings, and profits
were down. Michael Jordan, who was already being called the
best basketball player, had transformed the NBA into the
hottest operation in sports.

And there were the endorsements. In the first two years of
its contract with Michael Jordan, Nike sold $130 million dollars
worth of Air Jordans. The Nike deal had been just the first of the
agreements agent David Falk had negotiated for his client. Soon
Michael was popping up on television and in magazine ads and

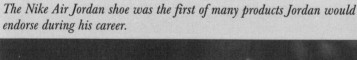

*The Nike Air Jordan shoe was the first of many products Jordan would
endorse during his career.*

on billboards for such huge companies as General Mills, Coca-Cola, and Wilson Sporting Goods. Michael Jordan was everywhere. Of course, the NBA was getting more popular now, but there was no question who was bigger. It was Michael Jordan without a doubt.

Chicago sportswriter Bob Greene in his book *Hang Time: Days and Dreams with Michael Jordan* described the Jordan phenomenon.

> On the television screen . . . , he would make a layup between three defenders to solidify the Bulls' lead, and the opposing coach would, in frustration, call a time-out, and WGN would break for commercials and suddenly there would be Jordan eating a bowl of Wheaties, there would be Jordan chomping down a burger at McDonald's, there would be Jordan sailing in slow motion past the moon on behalf of the Coca-Cola Company. It was all so heroically lighted and stirringly photographed and artfully produced—by the time the commercial interruption was over and WGN was showing a shot of Jordan on the basketball court again, he might as well have been Clark Gable or John Wayne among a group of mere game-players.[21]

"They Froze Me Out"

Fame had a price. The combination of Jordan's early success on the court, his lucrative endorsement contracts, and his status as the most popular player in the NBA (and perhaps in all of sports) caused a negative reaction against him among his fellow NBA players. The backlash started early. Jordan had such high visibility in his rookie season that fans voted him onto the 1985 NBA All-Star Team. It should have been a proud moment for Jordan, but it wasn't.

When Michael arrived at Indianapolis's Hoosier Dome for the contest, he discovered just how much the NBA's established stars disliked him and resented the ease with which he had already become basketball's biggest attraction. Even Michael's clothing added to their displeasure. The other All-Stars arrived

Pop Icon

Just as Michael Jordan helped to show that white fans and consumers could identify with a black celebrity, he also helped to bridge the gap between large companies (with public relations problems) and black audiences. Nelson George in *Elevating the Game* explained how this happened:

> Jordan became a Coca-Cola spokesman, according to Neva Richardson of Chicago's Burrell Advertising, the nation's largest Black-owned agency, because the company needed help. In the wake of the New Coke fiasco, the soda makers hooked onto Max Headroom as their new commercial symbol. Problem was, Black folks—a huge portion of Coke's market—hated the computer-generated talking head. Here came Mr. Jordan. "Michael Jordan legitimized Max with a Black audience," by interacting with him in a spot, according to Richardson.

> But Jordan's ultimate challenge was getting signed with Mickey Dee's. "It took Pro Serve a year to turn McDonald's around," the company's Bill Strickland says. Three times Ronald McDonald said no to Jordan, citing as the major impediment the fact that Jordan played a team sport in which individual identification wasn't as high as in boxing, tennis, or golf. But Pro Serve kept up the pressure, and as Jordan went from man to pop icon McDonald's bought in.

> With his well-honed talents, shrewd advisors, and carefully cultivated smile, Jordan had . . . gone beyond a boundary. On-court he is, in his time, the equal of the big O, Russell, Wilt, the Pearl, and Dr. J. Off-court, though, Jordan is something new, something peculiar to his time.

in their team uniforms. Michael had on a glitzy Nike warm-up suit. It just reminded the others of the money this rookie was making off his lucrative agreement with the sneaker company, and they resented it.

Some say that the Detroit Pistons' Isiah Thomas had talked to the other All-Stars before the game and they had agreed to freeze Michael out. Although he played twenty-two minutes, he got to take only nine shots. And when he got the ball he was too frustrated to do much with it, making only two field goals.

The entire incident embarrassed Jordan, who later said,

They were saying that I was full of myself and that I was cocky and that I had a bad attitude, and the truth of it was, all I was trying to do was to be like them. And they froze me out during the game, and they kept the ball away from me, and I kept hearing that they were saying those things about me. . . . And I was really shattered.[22]

But he wasn't too shattered to let it get him down. He planned to get his revenge on Isiah Thomas. The next Bulls game after the All-Star break was against Detroit. Michael played his heart out. No one was going to freeze him out now. He scored 49 points and grabbed 15 rebounds to help Chicago to a 139-126 overtime victory.

Yet even some of Jordan's own teammates resented his success. Their resentment was fueled by a simple fact. While Michael was leading the league in scoring and becoming world famous, he had not led the Bulls to any championships. To many in sports this "proved" he was hogging all the glory but not being a team player. A typical incident occurred in December 1990. Jordan got hot early in a game against the Indiana Pacers, scoring 20 points in the first quarter. But after that he cooled down considerably, scoring "just" 17 points in the rest of the game, which Chicago won easily—124-95. The next day a headline read "Jordan's Act 1 Does It for Bulls." Some of his teammates weren't too happy about that. "Talk to Michael," one of them snapped the next day, "he gets all the credit anyway."[23]

Changes were coming, however, for the Bulls. Soon there would be new management on the team and a new style of play for Michael Jordan—and a championship for Chicago.

Chapter 3

A Championship for Chicago

IT WASN'T JORDAN'S fault that the Bulls weren't winners. The rest of the team wasn't really championship caliber, and even a Michael Jordan couldn't create a championship team all by himself. In 1987–88, though, he started to get some help. The Bulls traded for draft rights to six-foot, seven-inch forward Scottie Pippen, a consensus All-American (a top player as chosen by sportswriters) at Central Arkansas University. That same year Chicago made Clemson's six-foot, ten-inch forward Horace Grant their first round draft choice. Neither was particularly impressive in his first pro season (Pippen scored 7.9 ppg, Grant just 7.7). But the next season each improved dramatically, and seven-foot, one-inch, 245-pound center Bill "Mr. Bill" Cartwright arrived in a trade from New York for power forward Charles Oakley. In particular, Pippen would eventually develop into one of the NBA's finest stars.

Just as important, however, was a personnel change that didn't involve a player. In 1989–90 Phil Jackson took over as Bulls head coach, replacing the intense Doug Collins. Jackson was a complex personality. His parents had been strict fundamentalist ministers who had taken a vow of poverty and forbade their son to enjoy such earthly pleasures as movies and dances. But in the 1960s, young Jackson embraced the counterculture of the time. He grew his hair long, listened to the Grateful Dead, and became a vegetarian. When he coached the Albany Patroons in the Continental Basketball Association, he lived in nearby Woodstock among many 1960s artists and musicians.

Jackson was an assistant to Collins during the 1988–89 season. One night Collins argued a referee's call and was ejected from a game, and Jackson took over. Ordinarily that wouldn't mean much. But Jackson did such a marvelous job that the Bulls players suddenly knew that Jackson—and not Collins—would be the right person to coach the Bulls.

Jackson's New System

Collins had built his entire team's offense around Michael Jordan. Phil Jackson wanted to develop a better-balanced offense. Jackson thought the team—and Jordan—could be more successful if Jordan scored a little less. When he took over the Bulls he put that strategy into effect, and he also instituted a more aggressive defense, turning both Jordan and Pippen loose on opponents.

Jordan had clashed with Doug Collins, and he was now more comfortable with Jackson's more easygoing approach, one that spent time with each player and tried to make everyone fit into the big picture. Jackson once revealed his coaching philosophy.

> I have to spend a lot of time thinking about people. I remember my dad thinking in terms of the congregation, and it was the pastor's responsibility to remember everyone, sort of like a shepherd with his flock, and I believe that about a team. You can't think of them as just players for a coach, but you have to think of them as a group and relate to them that way, even without words. Sometimes just a wink or a pat on the shoulder will do it.[24]

While Michael was happy with Jackson's personal style, at first he wasn't happy with taking fewer shots—and scoring fewer points. And he reacted by shooting at a wild pace at the beginning of each game, scoring huge numbers of points in each first quarter. He was clearly afraid Jackson's new system would lower his point total—and he wasn't happy about that. He was also afraid if he didn't shoot enough early in the game, he wouldn't be sharp enough to make the big shot later. "I can't go out and win games if I'm not in the flow," he complained to

Coach Phil Jackson hugs Jordan after a Bulls' victory. Jackson did not want Jordan to carry the team's offense; instead, he helped other players to excel so that the Bulls would be a well-rounded team.

Bulls assistant coach John Bach. "I just can't take twelve shots a game and then hit the winning shot."[25]

But as the Bulls began to win more, Jordan settled into Coach Jackson's new style of play. The Bulls were no longer a one-man team. Soon they would become a championship team.

Juanita

Off the court Michael had also formed a championship team. In February 1985 he had started dating Juanita Vanoy, a former model who was now an executive secretary with the American Bar Association. Michael had dated others, including actress

Michael and Juanita

Michael Jordan faces many pressures from playing in the NBA and in dealing with the stress of being a celebrity. A strong marriage helps him deal with those issues. Author Mitchell Krugel in *Jordan: The Man, His Words, His Life* revealed what the Jordans' marriage was like:

> So many times when the Bulls were on the road, the FTD man would ring the doorbell at Juanita and Michael Jordan's house. Another bouquet of flowers would come from Michael, a ritual he started when she was still Juanita Vanoy—the model from the south side of Chicago, whom MJ started courting when he was 22. Four years into their marriage—Michael's last season [before his retirement to take up baseball] on the long and grinding road of the NBA—the romance was even too mushy for a crowd-pleasing episode of "Love Connection."
>
> The day after the Chicago Bulls won their first NBA title (June 13, 1991), Juanita Jordan celebrated her 32nd birthday. . . . Earlier that day, Michael had given her two presents. One was a chance to hold the NBA championship trophy that he had hardly released since the Bulls won it 12 hours before; the other, a gold Cartier watch adorned with a band of rubies and gold.
>
> Later that day, Michael took her to a downtown photographer to have a portrait of them taken. While waiting for lights to be adjusted, film to be loaded into cameras, actually sitting still for a picture, Michael hugged and kissed his wife continuously. Their relationship was not without its scenes from a Harlequin romance novel.

Michael and Juanita flank their son Jeffrey.

Robin Givens (who would eventually marry boxer Mike Tyson) after joining the Bulls, but Juanita was different. She liked Michael for the person he was, not just because he was a star athlete. The two were first engaged on New Year's Eve 1987, but later decided to break it off—although they continued to see each other. In December 1988 they had a son, Jeffrey Michael Jordan. On September 2, 1989, Juanita and Michael were finally married. This new stability in his life would help Michael deal with the pressures of delivering a championship to Chicago.

The March to a Championship

As the 1990–91 season began Michael Jordan had already played parts of six seasons for the Bulls. He had established himself as the game's biggest star, but he had not delivered a championship. This season would be different.

It started out modestly, however, with Chicago winning just twelve of its first twenty games. Then the team caught fire, going 49-13 the rest of the way and finishing with a franchise-record sixty-one victories, including a team record twenty-six straight home wins. As usual, Jordan had a big part to play in the team's success. He led NBA scorers for the fifth straight season, with 31.5 ppg.

The Bulls finished first in the NBA Central Division and moved on to the Playoffs. In the postseason's first round, Chicago swept the Knicks in three games, taking game one by an NBA Playoff record of 41 points. Round two was a little harder—but only a little. The Bulls beat Charles Barkley and the Philadelphia 76ers 4-1, taking their only loss by just a two-point margin. In the final game, Michael singlehandedly finished off the 76ers, scoring the Bulls' last 12 points, including 8 after Philadelphia had rallied to score 13 points and tie the score. Jordan totaled 38 points for the game—with 19 rebounds.

In the Eastern Conference Finals, it was another Bulls sweep, as the team enjoyed taking revenge on its archrivals, Isiah Thomas and the Detroit Pistons. Jordan was clearly pleased that the Bulls had beaten the Pistons, a team with a long history of rough play.

"People are happy the game is going to get back to a clean game and away from the bad-boy image," Jordan said even before the series was over. "People don't want this kind of basketball, the dirty play, the flagrant foul, the unsportsmanlike conduct. It's bad for basketball."[26]

Making it all the sweeter was the fact that it was a true team effort—both on defense and offense. In the final game, the Bulls had five players scoring double figures—Jordan, 29, Pippen, 23, Grant, 16, Paxson, 12, and reserve forward Cliff Levingston, 10.

For the first time in their history the Bulls were in the NBA Finals. They were facing a team used to winning. The Los Angeles Lakers had captured NBA titles in 1986–87 and 1987–88 and reached the finals in 1988–89. Michael Jordan was also facing a challenge of his own. As the Finals began, sportswriters and fans were describing the Finals not as a matchup of two great teams—

"I Have Cleared the Way a Bit"

Michael Jordan possesses an almost unique ability to appeal to both white and black audiences. Some African-Americans have criticized him for not being more political or vocal about racial issues. But Jordan does take significant pride in his black heritage. Sally B. Donnelly's 1989 article in *Time* described one way that Jordan showed solidarity with his fellow African-Americans:

In 1986 Jordan went through a six-week initiation period to join a national black fraternity, Omega Psi Phi. Omega is the third oldest black fraternity in the country and has 700 chapters nationwide that coordinate social, political and business activities. Among its 80,000 initiates, Omega counts such notables as Jesse Jackson, N.A.A.C.P. director Benjamin Hooks and Philadelphia's Mayor Wilson Goode. "It is another sort of community for me," says Jordan. "It is an organization made up of men who want to give something back to society." An omega tattoo on the left side of Jordan's chest symbolizes his commitment to the fraternity.

Jordan does not see his support for Omega Psi Phi as detracting from his goal to be a role model for youngsters of all races. "I try to be seen as Michael Jordan the person, not as black or white," he says. "I guess I am a pioneer, and at some time I may come up against a racial barrier, but at least I have cleared the way a bit."

but as a battle between two great stars, Michael Jordan and Magic Johnson. Michael hadn't wanted to face the Lakers. He had wanted to take on the Portland Trailblazers, whom the Lakers had been playing in the Western Conference Finals. He didn't want the Finals to be viewed as Jordan versus Johnson; he wanted them to be seen as a battle of two teams.

"Total Satisfaction"

Game one was indeed a terrific battle between the two teams. The Bulls led 30-29 after one quarter and 53-51 at the half. But then Los Angeles slowed the game down, rattling the Bulls and building up a 75-68 lead going into the last quarter. Finally, the Bulls chipped away and even held a 91-89 lead with just thirty seconds to go. The Bulls looked to Michael to put the game on ice. They gave him the ball. He shot. He missed. Then Magic Johnson fired a pass to Sam Perkins. Perkins sank it for a three-point play. Now Los Angeles led 92-91.

Again it was up to Jordan. Unselfishly, he tried to pass, but failed. Then, with just nine seconds remaining, he shot from seventeen feet out. It looked like Air Jordan had done it again, but the ball kicked out of the hoop. Both teams battled furiously for the rebound. The Lakers' Byron Scott grabbed the ball, drawing a foul in the process. He made one of his two free throws. And that's where game one ended, with the score Lakers 93, Bulls 91.

Michael Jordan had 38 points, but he had failed in the clutch. He had proven he was human after all.

Game two saw Michael try a radical new strategy. As the game started he played point guard and barely shot at all. His teammates did, however. John Paxson, Scottie Pippen, Horace Grant, and Bill Cartwright made a remarkable 73.4 percent (47-for-64) of their shots in the game, and the Bulls led 48-43 at the half. In the second half, Jordan did shoot—and score. He went 15-for-18 and at one point hit 13 straight shots. Chicago coasted to an easy 107-86 win.

Game three was as great a game as game one—maybe better. The score was tied at 25-25 at the end of the first quarter. The Bulls held a razor-thin 48-47 lead at the half. Then the Lakers

Horace Grant outleaps Magic Johnson of the Los Angeles Lakers. When other teams concentrated on blocking Jordan, players like Grant took over the Bulls' scoring.

broke loose. They scored 12 straight points and built up a 67-54 lead. Michael was shooting poorly. But the Bulls still battled back, finally evening it at 74-all in the middle of the fourth quarter. With eleven seconds left Chicago pulled ahead 90-89. But then Lakers center Vlade Divac sank a bank shot and (after a foul call) a free throw. Now, Los Angeles was up 92-90 with just 10.9 seconds left.

There was no mystery about which Bull would get the ball—and shoot the ball. With 3.4 seconds on the clock Michael got the ball fourteen feet out and launched a jump shot that tied the game 92-all.

Now it went into overtime, and Jordan finished off the Lakers, making two layups and two foul shots to help Chicago to a 104-96 win. The Bulls were up two games to one.

Game four wasn't very exciting compared with the first three. Jordan scored 28 points in the Bulls 97-82 win. He could hardly wait to finish off the Lakers and enjoy his first title. "I can taste it and I can smell it," he said. "Maybe I'm overexcited. I'm anxious to go ahead and win it, but I have to be patient. I've been waiting seven years already." [27]

Michael had 30 points and 10 assists in game five (his fourth double double of the Finals), but he wasn't the star of the game. That honor went to Scottie Pippen. Pippen not only had the job of guarding Magic Johnson, he also broke through for 32 points.

The game, however, was tied 93-all with 3:54 left to play. Then John Paxson went to work. The Lakers left him almost unguarded. The other Bulls took advantage of the situation and passed off to him time and time again. Paxson collected 10 points as the Bulls pulled away to win 108-101.

On June 12, 1991, Michael Jordan and the Chicago Bulls were champions of the basketball world.

Jordan cried with happiness, saying,

> This means so much to us. Winning this championship is harder than anything I've ever done before in basketball, with all the ups and downs I've gone through this season and the mental approach that I've had to take into each game. We never gave up hope, and now that this team has become part of history, it's a very gratifying feeling for me.[28]

The Bulls had clearly played more as a team in winning their title. Michael Jordan had still led all playoff players with 31.5 ppg (with 11.4 assists and 6.6 rebounds) and captured Playoff MVP

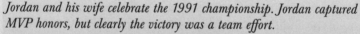

Jordan and his wife celebrate the 1991 championship. Jordan captured MVP honors, but clearly the victory was a team effort.

honors, but that 31.5 average was his lowest since his first play-off appearance back in 1985. Clearly, the Bulls' win was a team effort, as they held the mighty Lakers to a five-game series low of 458 points.

Now it was all over. Jordan had proved to the world he was more than a superstar. He was a winner. In the ecstatic pande-monium of the Bulls locker room he reflected on what it all meant, how important it was to him despite the money, endorsement contracts, and public acclaim he already had. He told reporters:

> It's total satisfaction. I always felt I played the style of basketball to win, but a lot of people didn't agree, say-ing I shot too much, scored too much. This is the time I've waited for. It's been a seven-year struggle for me, for the city and for the franchise, too. We started from scratch, we started from the bottom. I never gave up hope that this would happen.[29]

A Double Standard

The Bulls picked up in 1991–92 where they left off. They shattered their year-old team record of sixty-one victories, winning sixty-seven games (tying for the fourth-best record in NBA history).

But not everything about the season was positive. It was becoming clear that some members of the Bulls were unhappy with Jordan and with how team management and the NBA itself treated him. In his best-selling 1992 book *The Jordan Rules*, sportswriter Sam Smith painted a portrait of Jordan as still being a one-man team. Smith charged that Jordan was not the pleas-ant, smiling fellow shown in commercials—that he was really a selfish individual who did not enjoy good relations with his teammates, particularly with Bill Cartwright, Will Perdue, Steve Colter, and Brad Sellers.

The public might not have believed the stories in *The Jordan Rules*, except for Jordan's controversial actions in October 1991. Following their triumph in the NBA Finals, President George Bush invited the Bulls to the White House. It was a great honor for the team, but evidently Jordan didn't think so. He skipped the event. (Scottie Pippen charged that Michael would have gone if Bush had met with him alone.) Two days later, Jordan also skipped the team's mandatory media day and physical examination. It was beginning to appear that maybe Jordan really did think he was bigger than the team. Maybe he even thought he was bigger than the president of the United States. "There's dissension because he didn't show up at the White House, and now I think a lot of people are seeing there's a double standard," said Bulls forward Horace Grant. "I think a lot of guys [feel that way], but they're just keeping it to themselves." [30]

Not only the Bulls appeared to be applying a double standard when Michael Jordan was around. Some said the NBA was also favoring its star performer. Jordan's teammate John Paxson complained in the spring of 1991:

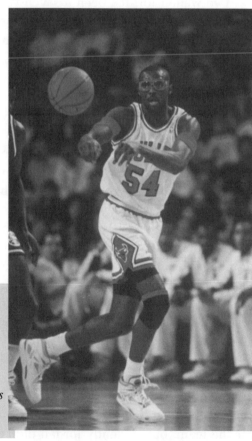

Horace Grant was one of the outspoken players who condemned Jordan for not attending a White House party given in the team's honor. Angered teammates accused the Bulls' managers of letting Jordan get out of team functions too easily.

We get a speech at the start of the season from the head of [NBA] referees [Darrell Garretson]. He tells us if Michael Jordan and John Paxson are doubleteaming a player and there's a foul on Michael Jordan, it'll go to John Paxson. We're in the entertainment business.[31]

Proving They Could Do It Again

Nonetheless, on the court, the Bulls put such controversy behind them. In late March 1993 Michael was on fire. Against the Washington Bullets he scored 51 points. Two games later he pumped in 50 against the Denver Nuggets. In the Bulls' next game (a 126-102 pasting of Cleveland) he poured in 44 more.

And the team around Jordan continued to grow even stronger. Chicago led the league with a .508 field goal percentage. Horace Grant averaged 14.2 points and 10.0 rebounds per game. Scottie Pippen in particular was turning into a gem. He averaged 21.0 points and 7.7 rebounds, started for the 1992 NBA All-Stars, and made the All-Defense First Team and the All-NBA Second Team. But the Bulls were more than Jordan, Pippen, and Grant. Coach Phil Jackson had a role for each member of the team. They were part of a well-designed machine, a machine designed to win games. Michael agreed with the philosophy. "When we started winning championships," said Michael, "there was an understanding among all twelve players about what our roles were. We knew our responsibilities and we knew our capabilities."[32]

Once again the Bulls went to the Playoffs. Now the pressure was on them to repeat—always a difficult task. Chicago swept the Miami Heat in round one, with Michael sinking 56 points in game three. The New York Knicks proved tougher in the Playoffs' next round. The Knicks took game six by a 100-86 margin to force a seventh game. New York fans taunted the Bulls, and it looked like Patrick Ewing, rather than Michael Jordan, might be going to the Finals. Even Jordan was unsure of himself, but he decided he had to stop worrying and just play his own game. In game seven, Michael exploded for 29 points in the first half, 42 points overall, and thoroughly outplayed Ewing. The Bulls defeated the Knicks 110-81.

Next stop was Cleveland and the Eastern Conference Finals, where the Bulls expected a much easier time than they had experienced against New York. But Michael came down with the flu and was severely weakened for game one. He scored just 20 points, and Chicago went down to its worst loss of the entire season, losing 107-81. But Jordan pumped in 46 points against the Cavaliers in game five, as the Bulls beat Cleveland in six games.

Now Jordan and the Bulls were again headed for the Finals. They would defend their NBA title against the Portland Trailblazers. Everyone was watching to see how Michael would match up against Portland's six-foot, seven-inch guard Clyde "The Glide" Drexler, whom many considered the NBA's second best player.

In game one, Drexler tried to outthink Jordan. He reasoned that since Michael had made just 27 of 100 three-point attempts during the regular season, he would give Jordan more room than normal outside. Drexler was wrong, dead wrong. Jordan tied two NBA records making six three-point shots and fourteen field goals in the game's first half. He also set a playoff record

with 35 points in that first half (beating Elgin Baylor's old mark of 33, set in 1962). The Bulls coasted to an easy 122-89 win, one of the biggest blowouts in NBA Finals history.

Game two should have been another easy Chicago victory. Instead, the team blew a four-minute, 10-

John Paxson (left) and Scottie Pippen (right) double-team Mark Jackson of the New York Knicks during the 1992 Eastern Conference Playoffs.

point lead as seven-foot Trail-blazers center Kevin Duck-worth launched a jumper to tie the contest at 97-97. With just seconds remaining, Michael got the ball. It was a moment made for him. He let loose with a long outside jump shot.

Clunk.

This was one Jordan mira-cle shot that never happened. He missed. The game went into overtime, and six-foot, five-inch Portland guard Danny Ainge got hot. He pumped in 9 points to fuel a 115-104 Trailblazers victory.

Clyde Drexler redeemed himself in game three, scoring 32 points, but the Bulls went for a more balanced offense (Jordan, 26 points; Pippen and Grant, 18 each) and Chicago won 94-84.

Jordan shoots over the head of Portland Trailblazer Clyde Drexler. After six games against Portland, the Bulls succeeded in snagging their second NBA championship.

Chicago led Portland all the way in game four, until the final 3:35 of the game, then couldn't put the Trailblazers away. They ended up losing to the Trailblazers 93-88, despite Jordan's 32 points.

The Bulls made up for that disappointment in game five, dispatching Portland by a 119-106 score. Michael was at the top of his game with 46-points, but the win was a team effort. Scottie Pippen came close to a triple double (scoring double digits in the three main statistics), with 24 points, 11 rebounds, and 9 assists. The Bulls as a team shot 55 percent from the field.

In game six, Portland held a commanding 79-64 lead after three quarters. It looked like they would take the Finals into a deciding seventh contest. Coach Phil Jackson thought about the situation. Conventional strategy dictated that he should go with his best.

Jackson, however, was never conventional. He left Michael Jordan—*and* Horace Grant *and* John Paxson *and* Bill Cartwright on the bench—and sent out Scottie Pippen and reserves Scott Williams, B. J. Armstrong, Bobby Hansen, and Stacey King. It was an incredible gamble. Either the Bulls' bench strength would be fresh and revitalize the team, or they would be outclassed by the Trailblazers and Jackson would be mercilessly second guessed.

Jackson guessed right—*incredibly* right. His "B" team of subs stunned Portland by outscoring them 14-2 and putting Chicago back in the game. Then Jordan came off the bench. He and Pippen were a two-man team, scoring the Bulls' last 19 points and putting Portland away for good. When the buzzer sounded, it was Chicago 97, Portland 93.

The Bulls were again NBA champions. Now came one more incredible challenge. Could Michael Jordan, Phil Jackson, and the Bulls "three-peat"?

Chapter 4

Three-Peat

W HEN A CHALLENGE faced Michael Jordan he accepted it. Sometimes he even took on an extra challenge just for fun.

After the Bulls captured their second straight NBA championship, the pressure grew for them to win three in a row, to "three-peat." Winning the championship and repeating three straight times was an incredibly difficult task for a sports team.

Baseball's New York Yankees had won five world championships in a row from 1949 through 1953, and coach Red Auerbach's legendary Boston Celtics finished first in the NBA every year from 1956–57 through 1964–65 and captured the Playoffs each season from 1958–59 through 1965–66. But times had changed in basketball—and in all of sports. It was tougher than ever to string together back-to-back titles, let alone to win three in a row. But now, Michael Jordan's critics were challenging him to further prove his greatness by "three-peating."

So Jordan had little time to rest on his laurels after Chicago's dramatic 1992 win over the Portland Trailblazers. He faced the pressure of winning again—and he faced an entirely new kind of challenge in the Olympic Games.

The Dream Team

Prior to 1992, only amateur athletes were allowed in Olympic competition. Those who had played a professional sport were banned from the games. Back in the 1912 Stockholm Olympics, America's Jim Thorpe won both the decathlon and the pentathlon. But when it was discovered that Thorpe had briefly played minor league baseball (which was not even an Olympic sport), he was stripped of his medals.

In 1992 all of that changed. Professional players could now compete. The United States (whose truly amateur team had lost in basketball to the highly-subsidized Soviet team in 1988) now could field a team composed of the brightest NBA stars (along with one token college star, Duke's Christian Laettner).

Many of the NBA's biggest names were on the team: Scottie Pippen, Phoenix Suns forward Charles Barkley, Utah Jazz forward Karl Malone, Utah point guard John Stockton, New York Knicks center Patrick Ewing, San Antonio Spurs center David Robinson, Golden State Warriors forward Chris Mullin, Portland Trailblazers forward Clyde Drexler. Even the Lakers' Magic Johnson came out of retirement to join the squad.

Michael Jordan wasn't sure he wanted to spend his summer at the Barcelona Summer Olympics. After each NBA season he needed a break from the tough physical and mental competition of high-level basketball. But eventually, the opportunity of starring in two Olympics—eight years apart—was too strong. The Dream Player joined the Dream Team.

Mobbed by Fans

Dream Team coach Chuck Daly thought his squad was a lot like a superstar rock group, with all the excitement a popular music tour generates. He was right. Wherever the Dream Team traveled, they were mobbed by fans. The fans knew this was the greatest aggregation of talent ever assembled on one team in the history of sports.

Even—maybe especially—opposition players were awed by the Dream Team. During one game, a player took time out from guarding Magic Johnson to wave to his team's bench. He had asked a teammate to snap a picture of him guarding the Laker superstar.

The Dream Team rolled over the opposition, over Angola (116-48), Germany (111-68), Brazil (127-83), and Spain (121-88). It won eight victories by a margin of 44 points. In the semifinals against a strong Lithuanian team—which featured six-foot, five-inch Golden State Warriors guard Sarunas Marciulionis—it rolled to victory by a gaudy 127-76 margin. Jordan didn't mind the lopsided nature of the games. In fact, he wanted his team to pour it on. "We want to destroy the opposition if we can," he commented. "We want people to remember that this is where the game was created."[33]

In the finals the United States faced Croatia, which boasted three NBA stars, six-foot, ten-inch Tony Kukoc (who many said was Europe's best player), six-foot, eleven-inch forward Dino Radja, and six-foot, five-inch shooting guard Drazen Petrovic. Coach Daly knew Croatia could be tough and didn't want his team suffering from overconfidence. To motivate the Dream Team he showed them a videotape of Team USA being upset

Chuck Daly coached the 1992 Dream Team. Though Daly knew he was coaching a winning team, he didn't want his players to be overconfident.

by the Soviet basketball team in the 1972 Olympics.

Daly must have had a premonition. The Dream Team came into the game playing poor defense. At one point Croatia led 25-23, the only time in the entire Olympics that Team USA trailed after the opening minutes. Then, the USA caught fire, outscoring Croatia 27-13 in the next seven minutes. In the opening minutes of the second half, the Dream Team outscored their opponents 11-2, with Jordan chipping in six of those points. Then came an 11-0 run, and the game was on ice. The final score: USA 117, Croatia 85.

"The Dream Team is so much better than everyone else," commented a stunned Petrovic, "but I still think it was good they were here. The Olympics are for the best and for everyone to see the best. Well, you saw the best, and, wow."[34]

Michael was truly pleased with the experience. "It was the most awesome feeling I ever had winning anything," he said when it was all over, "the most exciting thing I've ever been through. I got goosebumps all over my body."[35]

But controversy followed Jordan even at the gold medal ceremonies. The U.S. Olympic team was sponsored by Reebok—

Jordan sails above teammate Magic Johnson, preventing the Croatians from scoring.

and U.S. Olympians wore the Reebok logo on their warm-up suits. Michael Jordan, of course, had a lucrative contract with Reebok's rival Nike and wasn't about to promote Nike's big competitor. To get around that problem, Jordan and Charles Barkley (who also had a contract with Nike) draped American flags around their shoulders to hide the Reebok logo. "The American flag cannot deface anything," said Jordan. "I'm a person who feels that whatever you believe in, you stand up for it." [36]

Even before the incident, there was rumbling about Michael hoping to exploit the Olympics for Nike. "I hear Jordan wanted to take part in the opening ceremonies," joked syndicated columnist Scott Ousler, "but backed out when the USOC [United States Olympic Committee] denied him permission to wear a huge Nike shoe on his head." [37]

Three-Peat

As the Bulls reported to their training camp to begin taking their shot at the fabled "three-peat," there was trouble on the team. Michael's teammates began grumbling more and more about the special treatment he received from coach Phil Jackson, how he was excused from practices and events that every other team member was expected to attend. Horace Grant was so fed up he boycotted the camp for a few days in protest.

Jordan himself felt worn out, not only from playing competitive basketball all summer in the Olympics, but from the grind of years in college and NBA play. "I've never gone through anything like this in my career," he commented. "All my life, I've been playing basketball, and it's been a joy. But it isn't now. One day I'm fine. The next day I don't want to see a basketball."[38]

Phil Jackson may have granted Jordan a special favor or two but he had something planned that Jordan wouldn't like: slightly less playing time. Michael was now 29, and Jackson wanted him to be at his best when he was on the court, particularly late in the regular season and in the NBA Playoffs. As Jackson explained late in the 1992–93 season,

> Michael and I have met every year before the season and talked about what the season will be like and how we want to utilize him. This year, we knew his minutes and his scoring average would go down to save him for the crucial times of the game and the season. There was a lot of pressure on him early in the season when he wasn't scoring a lot, but he stuck through it and now it's paying off.[39]

During the gold medal ceremonies, Jordan, a Nike spokesman, draped the American flag over his Olympic uniform to hide its Reebok logo.

"The Driving Force"

Detroit Pistons' coach Chuck Daly coached the Dream Team in Barcelona. In his book *America's Dream Team: The Quest for Olympic Gold,* he described Jordan's greatness, a greatness that stood out even on that team:

> Michael's talents are almost indescribable. He has a small forward's body and the quickness of a guard. He has perhaps the most athletic quickness of anyone who has ever played in the NBA. He's got a complete offensive game—great moves to the basket, incredible leaping ability, and the touch of the best shooters from up to three-point range.

> Then you add what he's capable of doing defensively, both individually and within the team defense, and you have the complete package. . . .

> Then there are the intangibles—the competitiveness, wanting to win every time out. There are a lot of guys who have talent—they don't have Michael Jordan's talent, but they have talent—but they don't want to win badly enough, and so they give in to fatigue. He never gives in to fatigue, which is quite a gift.

> And he's a driving force on his team, a leader. Athletic basketball skills aren't enough to win in our league. So much of winning is mental. You have to have mental toughness along with the skills. I'm not sure that the rest of the Chicago players would reach the level that they have without Jordan as the driving force, motivating them on a day-to-day basis.

Michael Jordan wasn't scoring much early in the 1992–93 season, but the Bulls weren't winning much either. As late as January they still had a losing record. Both Jordan and Scottie Pippen were still tired from their Olympic adventures. Center Bill Cartwright was having difficulties with his knees. Veteran Bulls guard John Paxson was out with an injury.

Then the team caught fire, posting a strong second half and ending the regular NBA season with a fine 57-25 record. It was the third best record in the league, behind the Phoenix Suns and the New York Knicks. Michael Jordan was a big part of the Bulls season, leading the NBA (for the seventh straight season) with a 32.6 ppg average. And in January he reached a career total of 20,000 points. Jordan was only the eighteenth player in NBA history to reach that plateau, and he had done it in 620 games, the second quickest march to the 20,000 mark. The great Wilt Chamberlain had accomplished the feat in just 499 contests.

In the first two rounds of the postseason, it looked like a "three-peat" would be easier than anyone could have imagined. First the Bulls swept the Atlanta Hawks. Then they did the same to the Cleveland Cavaliers.

Then came some real opposition. The New York Knicks would make it interesting for the Bulls. The Knicks had the home court advantage in the first two games and won both, downing Chicago by scores of 98-80 and 96-91. It looked like the postseason might belong to seven-foot Knicks center Patrick Ewing, rather than to Air Jordan. But the next two games would be on the Bulls home ground. Even though Michael missed 15 of 18 field goal attempts in game three, he made 16 of 17 foul shots and scored 22 points as the Bulls bounced back and won 103-83. In game four he was at his peak, scoring 18 points in the third quarter alone and accounting for 54 points in the Bulls 105-95 win.

Michael was in no mood to show mercy to the Knicks. In game five he achieved another triple double (29 points, 14 assists, 10 rebounds) as the Bulls won 97-94. In game six he scored 25 points as the Bulls finished off New York 96-88. Chicago would now face the Phoenix Suns in the Finals. Phoenix, which posted an NBA-best 62 wins, featured both six-foot, seven-inch forward Cedric "Ice" Ceballos, who led the NBA with a .576 field goal percentage, and NBA MVP Charles Barkley. Barkley had just joined the Suns and from the very beginning of his time with Phoenix, he set his sights high. "Our goal," he boasted, "is to get three of them [NBA championship banners], and you don't get all three unless you get the first one. We didn't come here just to win the Pacific Division. At least, I didn't."[40]

Jordan vs. Barkley

But while Charles Barkley talked about three NBA championships as a long-term goal, the Bulls were close to making that dream a reality. All that stood between them and their plan were four wins over the Phoenix Suns.

Charles Barkley and the Phoenix Suns stood in the way of the Bulls' third NBA championship title.

Michael poured in 31 points as the Bulls coasted to a 100-92 victory in game one against Phoenix. Instead of enjoying his performance, however, Jordan seemed bothered by all the media attention and talked about retiring in the near future, maybe in a year or two. Many thought he was just mentally worn out from the combination of Olympic and NBA competition.

Game two was a harder battle. Michael just missed his third Playoff triple double, as he posted 42 points, 12 rebounds, and 9 assists, and Charles Barkley matched Jordan with 42 points of his own. But Chicago finally won 111-108, before 19,023 fans at the America West Arena. Despite the fact that the first two games of the Finals had been played in Phoenix, Chicago now enjoyed a 2-0 lead in the series.

Phoenix now had its back to the wall, and gamely forced the Bulls into triple-overtime in game three. Michael didn't play particularly well, missing 24 shots, and Phoenix won 129-121. He bounced back, however, in game four. He scored 55 points (21-for-37 from the field; 13-for-18 from the foul line) in the

Bulls 111-105 win. Putting together such a high total wasn't easy. Suns coach Paul Westphal started by using Richard Dumas to guard Jordan, then put Kevin Johnson and Dan Majerle on him. "I used all kinds of methods to beat the defense," Jordan said. "One thing led to another." [41]

Now, the Bulls needed just one more win to "three-peat." "I told my teammates that we have a chance to close this out right now," Jordan said after game four. "If anybody wants to go back to Phoenix, they're certainly going without me." [42] What Jordan meant was that he wanted to wrap the title up in five games. He simply wasn't interested in returning to Arizona. He wanted it over now. The Suns wouldn't go quietly, however. They won game five 108-98, forcing the Finals to return to Phoenix.

Game six went back and forth. As the game drew to a close, though, Phoenix worked out a 98-94 lead. Michael Jordan cut

Although the Phoenix Suns would drag the competition to six games, Jordan and the Bulls pulled off a "three-peat" and captured the 1993 NBA title.

that lead to two points, with a drive to the basket, followed by a leaping layup as he battled two Suns defenders. With just four seconds left, Phoenix led 98-96. If they held on to win, game seven would be played on their home court. Chicago gained possession again, inbounding the ball to Jordan, who passed to Scottie Pippen. Pippen fired a pass to Horace Grant, who was open near the basket. Grant was open, and a basket would tie the score, but he was playing for higher stakes. Out of the corner of his eye he noticed John Paxson—out beyond the three-point line—and unguarded. Grant whipped the ball to Paxson. Paxson launched a 25-foot jump shot. The ball went in. The buzzer sounded, and the Bulls were three-time champions.

Michael Jordan had again played a key role in the Finals. He had 246 points (second only in a six-game series to Laker Jerry West's 278 in 1965), 101 field goals (breaking West's six-game record of 96 set in 1965). He averaged 41.0 ppg. All that production won him his third Finals MVP. People immediately began talking about a "four-peat," but Jordan wasn't interested in such speculation. "Let's just enjoy this one," [43] he quietly told the press.

He would not have long to savor his victory, however.

Chapter 5

"The Desire Just Isn't There"

THREE-PEAT OR NO three-peat, basketball was no longer fun for Michael Jordan. The world's greatest basketball player had become a prisoner of his own talent and his own fame. Reporters peppered him with questions. Columnists pinned every Bulls defeat on him. If the team lost (or even won) and Jordan scored 40 points, he should have passed more. If they lost and he scored only 12, he should have scored more. "It's a catch-22 sometimes," Jordan said after his 55 points provided Chicago with a 3-1 lead over Phoenix in the 1993 NBA Finals. "If I shoot too much, they say I'm trying too hard. If I don't take it upon myself, we don't win." [44]

Long ago, Michael Jordan had also lost his privacy. Reporters and columnists wouldn't leave him alone. He couldn't go out on the street or to a movie or a restaurant without attracting crowds of fans and well-wishers. They wanted to see what the greatest basketball player of all time was like. They wanted to see the superstar who sold them sneakers and hamburgers and Gatorade. After a while Jordan stopped going out, except to media events or to business meetings. He had become a prisoner of his own fame.

After each game, Jordan couldn't just walk out of Chicago Stadium, hop into his car and go home. The adoring crowds were too big. They wanted too much of him. Security guards (who were off-duty Chicago police officers) plotted out five separate "escape routes" for him, signaling the chosen path on walkie-talkies. At each turn, after every door and every corridor he walked through, another security guard was there to protect him. His car would be running when he got outside. Michael would be running too, running from the price of fame. At first Michael had been amused by all the fuss and by the cloak-and-dagger aspect of it all. Now he just felt trapped.

Even simple things, things we take for granted, were a major problem. If he went to the dentist he couldn't go when his dentist had regular hours. Instead the dentist would schedule Michael on one of his off days or in the evening, when the office and waiting room would be empty. The same went for haircuts. When Michael first arrived in Chicago, he enjoyed going out for a haircut. It gave him a chance to meet people. But that soon changed. At first he started doing the same thing as he did with his dentist—going when the barbershop was otherwise closed. But even that became a problem, so he had barbers come to his home to shave his head. Eventually, that too created difficulties, so Michael Jordan bought a pair of electric clippers and learned how to do the job himself.

"He Doesn't Ever Go Out"

Shopping, particularly in big department stores during the crowded Christmas season, was also impossible. Occasionally, he could call a smaller specialty shop and have them open for him after hours.

He would have to sneak into movie theaters, going in last after the house lights had gone down. Of course, getting to the theater itself was also a problem. Michael told Chicago sportswriter Bob Greene,

> If a movie theater is part of a mall, sometimes the security guys will ask if I need help, and I'll say just getting to the car after the show is over. So they'll sit behind me during the movie, just in case, and after it's finished they'll walk me back to the car.[45]

Even buying gas was a problem. Jordan was afraid to get out of the car for fear of attracting a crowd. So he only went to full-service stations.

It's the Shoes

Celebrity has its costs—a loss of privacy, a loss of freedoms, a sense of being a prisoner no matter where you go. In Mitchell Krugel's *Jordan: The Man, His Life, His Words,* Jordan revealed what a simple trip to the mall could be like—if you happen to be Michael Jordan:

How did life ever get this crazy?

Now, we're looking to buy a pair of shoes. You know how you would do it—go to a mall, look around, try on a few pairs. Maybe look in a few stores, try on a few more pairs and when the shoe fits. . . . Well, we're in the mall, but there's no time for browsing. We—we also being my assistant George Koehler, who I need with me for protection whenever I'm out in public—go into one store, we find a pair of shoes, and we buy them. Then, we get ready to leave.

Only as we're walking out the door, two teenage girls scream, "That's Michael Jordan." Next thing you know 300, maybe 400 people have gathered outside and backed us into the store. George had to get the owner to lock the door. People are asking to come in to buy a pair of shoes, but as George will tell you, they just want to be in the same room with Michael Jordan. The owner can't even unlock the door. George looks for a back door. There isn't one, so we have to go out the front. George calls mall security, and a couple of guards come to the rescue.

They form a ring, put me in the middle, and we make a run for it. George says to be careful not to hurt anybody, but they're all grabbing at me like a bunch of little John Starkeses [a tough member of the New York Knicks]. People are asking for autographs but you can't even think about stopping because it would turn into a mob scene.

"The one thing that's weird about Michael is that whenever we're together," Charles Barkley once observed, "we're in a hotel room because he doesn't ever go out."[46]

Part of the reason he opened Michael Jordan's, his own Chicago restaurant, in 1993 was so he could eat out whenever he felt like it and not have to call ahead so advance preparations could be made. Of course, he still ate in a fishbowl existence, eating separately from his customers in a special glassed-in dining area. But at least he could go out. Commenting sadly, Jordan said,

You know that commercial I made for Nike, about what if I was just another basketball player? What if my face wasn't on TV every five seconds? Well, that wasn't done just to sell shoes. That's how I really felt. There came a time when I just wanted to be another basketball player. And you know I couldn't.[47]

But Jordan was worrying about more than a lack of privacy. He was also concerned about his family's safety. He started carrying a laser-sighted pistol and spent heavily on installing a new security system for his son's school.

The Press

The press had also become a problem, part of the grind. Michael had certainly conducted interviews with almost as much skill as he used on the hardwood. He knew what to say and how to say it. He gave out good quotes for reporters, and they in turn took care of him, helping to build his image—an image that translated into millions of dollars worth of endorsement deals. But the same ques-

Jordan and his wife sample food at the opening of his restaurant in Chicago. Jordan went into the business partly because he could no longer eat in public without being mobbed by fans.

tions followed each game: Did he score too much? Was he helping the team? Was he running the team? And books came out that told about Jordan's relationship with his teammates and the resentment they felt about the special treatment the Bulls gave their superstar. *The Jordan Rules* by *Chicago Tribune* sportswriter Sam Smith particularly annoyed Jordan. It painted him as less than the flawless human being he was often portrayed as being. Smith said in an interview,

> The message of my book was to show that Jordan was human, not the perfect guy pictured in the ads. I found him to be a charming guy, fun to be around, but filled with human flaws. At times he was selfish, arrogant, but always celebrated. And in America, we excuse so many things for celebrity.[48]

Jordan didn't buy what Smith was saying. He thought Smith and similar reporters were out to get him. He began to complain about the treatment he was now getting from the press:

> I understood what dealing with the media was all about, and learning that was part of my education and maturity. Sometimes I wished I wasn't the only one on our team who did most of the talking. But sitting with the media was just my nature, part of my personality. I never wanted them to think of me as a rude type of guy. It took a little bit of experience to understand matters.
>
> They all had a job to do, just like I had a job to do. But they didn't have any sympathy for normal people sometimes. I didn't appreciate that. I never minded them printing the specifics, but opinions the columnists used to have bothered me sometimes. They were the guys who had no sympathy. You couldn't have paid me enough to do their job.[49]

"Five-Card Charlie"

In the early 1990s Michael Jordan began to face more embarrassing questions than those concerning his basketball scores. Jordan was a fierce competitor and one way he continued to compete while off the basketball court was by gambling, either on golf matches, or in casinos. Reporters and NBA officials began to wonder if Jordan was gambling too much—and if the superstar with the squeaky-clean image was associating with the wrong kind of people.

One of those people was convicted cocaine dealer James "Slim" Bouler. Back in October 1991, when Jordan had made headlines by skipping the team's trip to the White House to meet President George Bush, he told everyone he couldn't attend because he was taking time with his family.

That wasn't true at all. Instead Jordan joined Bouler for a weekend of $10,000-per-hole rounds of golf matches. Later, government investigators had found a check for $57,000 from Jordan in Bouler's possession. For over a year Jordan claimed it had been

Off the court, one of Jordan's hobbies is golf. His proclivity to wager during friendly golf matches, however, brought him notoriety when some of his large losses were made public.

for an investment in a driving range. When Bouler went to trial on money laundering charges in October 1992, Jordan was called to the witness stand. Michael was not a target of the investigation. In some sense the defense even treated him like the celebrity he was, at one point asking, "Are you the guy on the Wheaties box?"[50] But Jordan still had to answer some difficult questions. The prosecution forced him to admit he had not been telling the truth about the money that had changed hands between him and Bouler. He had to admit he had not *invested* $57,000, he had *lost* $57,000 gambling with a convicted cocaine dealer.

Jordan was clearly embarrassed taking the witness stand under such circumstances—and admitting under oath that he had lied about his gambling losses. "Winning is great," Jordan said about his gambling, "but when you lose that amount and get all the abuse I got, it ain't worth it any longer. If any problems occur on this team, it won't be because of me. I won't compete on the golf course again."[51] But many of Jordan's associates doubted that he really had learned his lesson.

One associate was bail bondsman Eddie Dow, who had served as the "banker" (that is the individual who held the stakes) during Michael's golf weekend with "Slim" Bouler. In February 1992 Dow was shot to death in Gastonia, North Carolina. In Dow's briefcase, police found photocopies of checks written by Michael Jordan. The checks totaled $108,000, and Dow's brother said they were written, at least in part, to cover more Jordan gambling losses.

More Criticism

In May 1993 Jordan's gambling attracted more criticism. Newspapers revealed that on the night before a Playoff game at Madison Square Garden against the Knicks, he drove down to Atlantic City and was out gambling at the Bally Grand casino until 2:30 the next morning. Jordan claimed he left the casino at 11:00 P.M. and was in bed by 1:00 A.M. He scored 36 points the next night in the Bulls 96-91 loss.

In June 1993 another friend of Jordan, a San Diego businessman named Richard Esquinas, published a book called *Michael & Me: Our Gambling Addiction . . . My Cry For Help!* In that book Esquinas charged that at one point in 1991 Jordan owed

In 1993 two teenagers shot and killed James Jordan because they wanted to steal his $50,000 automobile.

him $1.25 million for losses on ten days of golf matches and that he and Jordan later negotiated the debt down to $300,000. Jordan denied he had lost $1.25 million, but he did admit to gambling with Esquinas. Jordan attested, "Because I did not keep records, I cannot verify how much I won or lost. I can assure you that the level of our wagers was substantially less than the preposterous amounts that have been reported." [52]

Heavy gambling even took place among the Bulls themselves. In 1989, card playing among players (including Jordan and Scottie Pippen) had reached a serious point. While they were waiting for their commercial flights, they would sit in airport gate areas, with thousands of dollars in hundred-dollar bills between them. The team's response was not to make them stop, but instead to charter private planes for their flights—so no one could see the team's high-stakes gambling. As more and more stories leaked out about Michael's gambling—and about his unsavory associates— Horace Grant (and even Pippen) started making fun of Jordan, calling him "Scarface" and "Five-Card Charlie." [53]

Tragedy

In July 1993 tragedy entered Michael Jordan's life. Jordan's father James had remained remarkably close to his superstar son. When Michael had signed his first pro contract, James had retired from General Electric and spent a great deal of time with Michael as he dealt with the pressures of his career. When the gambling allegations emerged, it was James Jordan who often served as Michael's public spokesman.

That summer, James Jordan was returning to his home in the Raleigh area from a funeral in Wilmington. He was alone and tired and pulled his car—a red $50,000 Lexus 400 with license plates "UNC 23" that Michael had bought him—off U.S. Highway 74 near Lumberton, North Carolina, to take a short nap. Shortly thereafter, two eighteen-year-olds, Larry Demery and Daniel Green, spotted the car. They thought they would steal it. When they saw James Jordan in the car, they panicked and shot him once in the chest. James Jordan was dead at age 56.

At first Michael Jordan wasn't too concerned that his father was missing. "He would go off on his own a lot," he remarked.[54]

Larry Demery (above) and Daniel Green (left) murdered James Jordan and dumped his body in a creek near the North Carolina border.

But when the car was found stripped outside Fayetteville, North Carolina, Michael and his family began to worry. Later South Carolina police analyzed the dental records of a body they had found in a snake-infested creek just across the North Carolina border. The records matched those of James Jordan.

The news hit Michael Jordan hard. So did the ugly—and often ridiculous—rumors that soon emerged. Some said James Jordan had been involved in a botched drug deal. One source even claimed that he was still alive, and had faked his own death. The rumors were false but added to the tremendous pain the Jordan family was already feeling.

Those rumors ended when police apprehended Demery and Green, suspects so stupid that they drove the flashy stolen Lexus to Green's mobile home, so stupid they videotaped each other with some of the possessions they had stolen from James Jordan.

"The Desire Just Isn't There"

After Michael had led the Bulls to the first NBA Championship in 1991, James Jordan urged his son to leave basketball and return to his first sport—baseball. Michael didn't. Instead the Bulls captured two more titles. But after James Jordan's death, Michael began to take his father's advice more seriously.

On October 6, 1993, he announced his retirement from the NBA. "I just feel I don't have anything else to prove," he told shocked reporters at a packed forty-minute press conference. "The desire just isn't there."[55] Before the press conference, he had met in an emotional session with his teammates, but as he spoke to the press he was almost drained. He spoke calmly and evenly. This was what he wanted to do, what he felt he *had* to do.

When Jordan announced his retirement, he led just about every Chicago Bulls statistical category, with 21,541 points scored, 8,079 field goals made, 3,935 assists, 5,096 free throws made, and 1,815 steals. He had scored 40 or more points in 135 games. His lifetime points per game average of 32.3 was the highest ever in the history of the National Basketball Association. Just one other player—the great Wilt Chamberlain (30.1)—had more than a 30.0 ppg career average. And even though Jordan had played in just nine pro seasons, his 21,541 points ranked

In 1993 Jordan announced that he was retiring from professional basketball. At a press conference, he told reporters that he no longer felt he had "anything else to prove."

fifth in NBA history. In seven of those nine seasons he had led the NBA in scoring—tying a record set by Chamberlain.

The Bulls—and all basketball—would have a tough time replacing Michael Jordan. And Michael Jordan would have a tough time replacing the NBA.

Chapter 6

A League of His Own

AFTER ANNOUNCING HIS retirement Jordan told the massive crowd of reporters who surrounded him, "I'm going to watch the grass grow, and then go cut it."[56] But relaxing wasn't his style. Some thought Jordan would take up golf—a game he had grown to love—and join the pro tour. He possessed a six handicap, shooting in the mid- to high-70s for eighteen holes.

Michael Jordan *would* take up a new game—but it wouldn't be on the links. Shortly after announcing his retirement Michael Jordan began to follow a very improbable dream. He was now thirty years old and had not played baseball seriously for almost fifteen years. But it had been his first love, and his late father had always cherished the idea that Michael would star on the diamond. In July 1993 Jordan even appeared at a celebrity event before Baseball's All-Star Game. Competing against such stars as Patrick Ewing, actor Tom Selleck, TV commentator and ex-NFL receiver Ahmad Rashad, Jordan banged out the most hits and won $8,600 for his favorite charity. At the time Michael denied he was interested in a baseball career "It ain't for me," Jordan joked to Cincinnati Reds All-Star shortstop Barry Larkin. Then he pointed at Ahmad Rashad and boasted, "But I beat him."[57]

A New Game

After leaving basketball, however, he began to change his tune. That October Jordan began to work out with Jim Darrah, the athletic director with the Illinois Institute of Technology. Darrah was no stranger to coaching celebrities in how to play baseball. Earlier he had coached Madonna and Tom Hanks for their roles in the movie *A League of Their Own*, a film about women's professional baseball in the 1940s. Now Darrah would be coaching Michael Jordan for his real-life role in professional baseball. "My father thought I could be a major league baseball player," Jordan remarked after one of these workouts with Darrah, "And I'm sure right now he can see me trying. I'm sure he's watching every move I make." [58]

Bulls owner Jerry Reinsdorf also owned baseball's Chicago White Sox. Jordan turned to Reinsdorf to make his dream come true. In December 1993 Michael began showing up at Comiskey Park, home of the White Sox, to take batting practice. Jordan and White Sox general manager Ron Schueler denied Jordan would ever sign with the Sox. After all, not everyone gets to play major league baseball—particularly without having played *any* baseball for fifteen years. "I'm just having a good time," said Jordan, "I'm trying to see how good I am. I'm hitting off the [pitching] machine. I'm just going through the phases, trying to see how

good I can get. . . . I'm not committing to anything." [59]

Jordan went skiing over the Christmas holidays but as January 1994 began, he was back at Comiskey Park, hitting against the pitching machine for two or three hours each day. Now the White Sox were keeping Michael's activities a secret, but rumors began flying that he was serious about launching a baseball career.

Jordan trains with the White Sox prior to their 1994 season. At this point, few people could guess whether Jordan was seriously considering a career in baseball.

"I've Never Been Afraid to Fail"

The media—and many professional baseball players—were skeptical about Jordan's chances. In fact, they were beyond skeptical. They thought the idea was ridiculous. "He's got two chances," scoffed disgraced baseball star Pete Rose, "And Slim just left town." [60]

Such talk did not discourage Michael Jordan. It only made him more determined to succeed, to become a ballplayer and to fulfill his father's—and his—dream. "I love to hear them say [things like] that," he confided to one reporter. "My whole life, that's been the kind of thing that has driven me. You tell me that I can't do something, and I'm going to do it." [61]

He continued to explain what was motivating him in this unlikely career move. "I've never been afraid to fail," said Jordan. "That's something you have to deal with in reality. You're not always going to be successful. I think I'm strong enough as a person to accept failure. But I can't accept not trying." [62]

On March 3, 1994, the White Sox opened their exhibition season. Jordan entered the game as a defensive replacement in

Cheers in His Dreams

Michael Jordan and his father had long dreamed that Michael might have a successful baseball career—in some cases literally. Bob Greene, in his book *Rebound: The Odyssey of Michael Jordan* described one of those dreams:

> I reminded him of a conversation we'd had at the height of the Bulls' championship years. He had said that in the dreams he had when he was asleep at night, he heard cheers. But in those dreams, he was not a basketball star. He was a baseball player—in the dreams, he was a pitcher. He had said the cheers he heard in his dreams were different from the cheers he heard in real life, in arenas around the NBA. The basketball cheers he heard every NBA night were almost ordering him to be good. In those odd baseball dreams, he said, the cheers were cheers of hope. They sounded different to him. In the baseball dreams, the people in the stands didn't know anything about him, didn't know if he had the talent to succeed, but they were on his side anyway.

> And now he was about to step into that dream.

Jordan is caught in a rundown between bases during one of the White Sox exhibition games. Because of the many errors he made on the field, the Sox dropped Jordan and sent him to a Double-A farm team.

the bottom of the fifth. In the next inning he came to bat and bounced a grounder back to Rangers pitcher Darren Oliver. Oliver took a swipe at Jordan as he sped by, then threw to first just to be sure. Home plate umpire Drew Coble called Jordan out on Oliver's tag, but first base umpire Chuck Meriweather called him safe at first. Coble's call stood; Michael Jordan was out.

"As much as I wanted to be safe," Michael told reporters after the game, "I knew I was out. The ref at first confused me."[63] The ref? Jordan's use of basketball terminology made his critics jeer even louder. "Bag it, Michael!" headlined *Sports Illustrated* on its cover, "Jordan and the White Sox Are Embarassing Baseball."[64] It was quite a comedown. Just two years before Michael had been *SI*'s "Sportsman of the Year." Except for Muhammed Ali no one had been on *SI*'s cover more often. The magazine had even used Michael Jordan highlight videos to sell subscriptions. Now it was mocking him.

Jordan went just 3-for-20 (a .150 batting average) in spring training. His fielding was also shaky. One afternoon he botched an easy fly ball. The error embarrassed Jordan. The next morning, he told a reporter,

I went to bed around 9 last night. I kept replaying it in my mind. I kept seeing the ball coming to me, and I was replaying it over and over. . . . I couldn't stop seeing it. Easy! I should have had it. I woke up at 3:30 in the morning, and I was still thinking about it. I didn't want to see it, but it was all I could see.[65]

Move to the Minors

The White Sox couldn't justify keeping Jordan on their roster. They could not even justify sending him to the next highest level of professional baseball, Triple-A. Instead they sent him to their Double-A farm club, the Southern League's Birmingham Barons.

Jordan faced a big adjustment in the minors. He'd no longer be facing stars like Patrick Ewing or Charles Barkley. Instead he'd be competing against players like Chattanooga Lookouts first baseman Tim Belk or Jacksonville Suns catcher Chris Widger—players few persons had ever heard of—or would ever hear of. And he would have trouble being even as good as they were.

Jordan would no longer fly to New York or Los Angeles. Instead he'd be riding a bus to Knoxville or Memphis. "I'm not too adjusted to royalty that I can't ride a bus as long as it's a luxury bus,"[66] he joked in spring training. At Birmingham, he found out there were no luxury buses in the minors. So he looked into *buying* one—a $350,000 luxury bus like the ones used by touring rock or country music stars. It seated 35, boasted six televisions, a VCR, and even a wet bar in the back of the bus. Actually, despite all the news stories that appeared saying Michael had purchased the bus, he hadn't. Eventually, a charter bus company ended up letting the Barons lease the new luxury bus at no extra charge because of the publicity they would receive.

Even Michael Jordan couldn't buy, lease—or borrow—base hits. Not even singles. He continued to struggle at bat. In May, Jordan considered quitting the team, but manager Terry Francona, a former major league outfielder (and a future manager of the Philadelphia Phillies), talked him out of it.

Nonetheless, Jordan was the best drawing card the Southern League had ever seen. The Barons finished dead last in the league's Western Division but still led the circuit by drawing a club record 467,867 fans (an average of 6,983 fans per game). That was up from 277,096 the previous year when the club had finished first. The next best attendance in the league in 1994 was just 319,279. Games featuring Jordan, both at home and on the road, accounted for 39 percent of all attendance in the ten-team Southern League. Twice Chattanooga drew nearly 17,000 fans when Jordan came to visit. Southern League president Jimmy Bragan observed,

> You know, we've had Cal Ripken and Jose Canseco and Bo Jackson and Mark Langston and everybody else come through this league. But like I was telling Michael, there's never been a player that had the effect on attendance that he has.[67]

Jordan showed little improvement while playing with the Birmingham Barons. His popularity, however, drew tremendous crowds to the games.

"The Biggest Thing to Hit Town"

When Michael Jordan turned to playing minor league baseball, it was big news across the nation's sports pages. And it was even bigger news in the ballparks of baseball's Southern League. Jim Patton's *Rookie: When Michael Jordan Came to the Minor League* recounted what all the excitement was like:

> In Jacksonville, the *Florida Times-Union* trumpets Michael's arrival in nearly every section. The front-page Michaelmania piece says the Jacksonville Suns, averaging 3,100 fans at home, expect to fit 10,000 into 8,200-seat Wolfson Park for each of these games, including roped-off standing-room areas. The club has ordered more that a ton of hot dogs, four times the typical order. . . .
>
> The sports section, of course, is bursting with Jordan plus all the details about tonight's starting times, tickets, you name it. A big headline, "AIR of confidence": a big color picture; a long piece that goes on to cover reminiscing about famous players who've appeared in Jacksonville—Babe Ruth, Ty Cobb, Christy Mathewson, Mickey Mantle, Denny McLain—as well as other luminaries who've come to town—Elvis, Sinatra, Liberace, Michael Jackson, the Beatles. Page eight is all Michael Jordan: a huge color caricature, a brief biography, a chart of his game-by-game fortunes so far, a sidebar about current prices on Jordan collectibles.
>
> Michael would certainly appear to be the biggest thing to hit town since John, Paul, George, and Ringo.

On July 11 the Southern League held its annual All-Star Game. Jimmy Bragan asked Jordan if he would consider playing in it. Bragan had to admit Jordan wasn't a true All-Star. He was third from the bottom in batting average among Southern League regulars, led all league outfielders in errors and had stolen just twenty bases in thirty-two attempts. But Bragan wanted to honor Jordan for boosting Southern League attendance. Jordan knew he didn't deserve to be an All-Star, and besides he wanted to spend a few days at home with his family. He turned Bragan down.

Making Progress

Michael continued to flounder after the All-Star break, but some observers thought they saw possibilities in his performance. Said Blue Jays minor league batting instructor Bill Buckner,

He was very raw early in the year, and he's come around a lot, but it's gonna take another year of Double-A. . . . He's got a chance to make the major leagues, but I'd say he needs at least a thousand more at-bats—winter ball, more minor-league ball. It depends on what kind of commitment he wants to make.[68]

Buckner was right. Jordan did begin to make progress. He was hitting under .200 at the All-Star break—and fell further below that mark during the month of July. But in August he finally began to feel comfortable at the plate. He batted .260 that month (and .304 in his last fifteen contests) and raised his average to .202 with three homers, 51 runs batted in and 30 stolen bases.

"When I saw him in August, he looked like a baseball player," said Steve Wulf, who had written the *Sports Illustrated* cover story mocking him in the spring. "He had a terrific swing and he was hitting the ball on the screws [solidly]. I'm a skeptic who's been convinced."[69]

After the Southern League season ended on Labor Day, the White Sox sent Michael to the Florida Instructional League. There he spent three weeks working hard on improving his fundamentals. From there it was on to the Arizona Fall League. This league was for the six top prospects in each organization. Jordan wasn't one of those half dozen, but the Sox got permission for him to attend anyway—and he continued to improve, hitting a respectable .252.

"People thought I'd embarrass myself, and that hasn't happened," Jordan said after the Arizona Fall League season concluded, "And now I'll go to spring training with a lot more confidence. I'm not going to feel lost this time."[70]

Confidence was also growing in the White Sox front office. It was announced Jordan would be sent to the Nashville Sounds of the Triple-A American Association in 1995. Jordan was ready for the move. He paid $17,500 to join a Nashville country club and rented a house in that city. Nashville Sounds president Larry Schmittou theorized that Jordan could easily earn a promotion to the White Sox when major league rosters expanded after September 1 of that season. Schmittou, however, was obviously thinking more of the attendance boom Jordan could set off in Nashville. Even Nike was planning to film a TV commercial with the former NBA star in a Sounds uniform. Other American Association teams also hoped to cash in, selling "Jordan ticket packages" before the Sounds—and Michael Jordan—would visit their own ballparks.

Strikebreakers and Parking Lots

But Jordan, and all of baseball, was facing a massive problem as the 1995 season approached: there might not *be* a 1995 season. In August of 1994 major league players had gone on strike, a strike that dragged on and caused the cancellation of the 1994 World Series. As spring training approached there was little movement toward a settlement. Players remained on strike, and owners talked of using replacement players—minor leaguers and marginal free agents—to fill major league rosters. These replacement players were viewed by many as strikebreakers and were widely disliked. Some thought Michael Jordan might become one of them, but both he and the White Sox denied that possibility. Instead, Jordan would report to the Sox minor league camp and avoid the stigma of being a replacement player.

That was the plan, but as the strike dragged on White Sox general manager Ron Schueler felt more and more pressure to attract fans to the Sox spring training camp. One day he approached Jordan on the subject. He didn't make a direct request that Jordan become a replacement player—but he came very close. Too close for Jordan.

An hour later, Michael Jordan had cleaned out his locker and left the White Sox minor league camp. His baseball career was over. Jordan later described his reaction to Schueler's request:

> I was disgusted. "Disgust" is a more accurate word than "anger." What had I done for the last year, other than to work as hard as I could, and to do everything I was asked to do? The one promise that was made to me was that they wouldn't put me in the position of being a strikebreaker—that if there were games in spring training that would be considered strikebreaker games, I wouldn't be asked to play in them.[71]

Something else was bother-ing Michael. The White Sox had adopted a rule that only those playing in the "major league"

Jordan quit the minor leagues because he felt the White Sox management was pressuring him to become a strikebreaker.

games could park in the official team parking lot. Michael, because he was playing with the minor league, had to park else-where. That might not seem like much—and to most players it wouldn't be. But to Jordan—surrounded always by fans and autograph seekers—it was a problem. He didn't want special favors from management—but he wanted a little cooperation, and he couldn't get it. Jordan revealed,

> I wasn't going to say anything to Schueler about it. I tried my best not ever to ask him for special treatment. But after a year, if he didn't know my situation . . . if he really didn't know what would happen if he kept me out of the players' parking lot. . . . If he didn't know, then that told me something. . . . Either way, I had to get out of there.[72]

"Mr. Jordan Loves the Challenge"

Baseball wasn't Michael Jordan's only non-NBA sports option. In February 1994 boxing promoter Dan Duva offered Jordan $15 million to fight the winner of the Evander Holyfield–Michael Moorer heavyweight title bout. According to the February 23, 1994, issue of the *Chicago Tribune*, Duva wrote to Jordan's agent, David Falk:

> This offer is not a joke. We are 100 percent serious. It seems that Mr. Jordan loves the challenge of proving he is the best, regardless of the sport. . . . I would like to offer Michael the ultimate individual sport challenge, an opportunity to fight for the heavyweight championship of the world. While this idea might seem crazy, remember, in the '60s Muhammad Ali and Wilt Chamberlain were close to finalizing arrangements for Wilt to challenge Ali for the world heavyweight championship. The deal fell apart when Ali backed out.

On March 3, 1995, in a short, prepared statement Michael Jordan broke the news to the world that his baseball career was over:

> As a 32-year old minor leaguer who lacks the benefit of valuable baseball experience during the past 15 years, I am no longer comfortable that there is meaningful opportunity to continue my improvement at a satisfactory pace.[73]

Now the question was: would he return to the Bulls?

Chapter 7

"I'm Back"

As soon as Michael left the White Sox camp, people wanted to know: would he be returning to the Chicago Bulls?

His homecoming would mean more than just the return of a supremely talented player. It meant big, big money for all sorts of people. It certainly meant more revenue for the NBA. It's TV ratings had dipped in the 1993–94 season, which he had missed entirely. And they continued to fall in the 1994–95 season. Michael Jordan back in uniform could reverse that trend. His return could also mean more money for all the companies with which Jordan had endorsement contracts.

Jordan wanted to know a few things about the Bulls before he returned. The Bulls were no longer the dominant team he once knew. In the 1993–94 season (led by Scottie Pippen, Horace Grant, B. J. Armstrong, and former Olympic star Tony Kukoc) they finished with a strong 55-27 record but failed to win the NBA Central Division. They did make the Playoffs but lost the Eastern Conference semifinals to New York. So far in the 1994–95 season they were having trouble even getting a winning record (as late as March 4 they were 29-30). Would coach Phil Jackson be coming back after the 1994–95 season? What were the team's plans for keeping Pippen? Jordan had to be sure the Bulls were committed to winning before he committed himself to a comeback.

Soon he had the answers he wanted. Both Jackson and Pippen were part of the Bulls' long-term plans. Jordan began practicing with the team, practicing hard, running wind sprints—and taking charge of the team's offense. "No one runs lines [wind

"A 32-Year-Old Minor-Leaguer"

When Michael Jordan gave up his baseball career and returned to the NBA, this is the statement he released to the press—and to the sports world (as quoted in the *Chicago Tribune*, March 11, 1995):

> Playing professional baseball has been a life-long dream, and for the past 18 months I have been dedicated to realizing that dream.
>
> When I began my baseball career, I set high standards for myself, as I have throughout my entire professional sports career. I knew the challenge would be difficult, and I also knew some would question my decision to pursue a career in baseball. But I committed myself to baseball for as long as I felt I was progressing in a positive direction and at a satisfactory pace. . . .
>
> I firmly believe that I have made considerable improvement as a baseball player, and the Chicago White Sox have substantiated my belief. Unfortunately, however, the labor dispute in Major League Baseball has made it increasingly difficult to continue my development at a rate that meets my standards.
>
> As a baseball fan, I sincerely hope the players and owners will satisfactorily resolve their disagreement as quickly as possible. As a 32-year-old minor-leaguer, who lacks the benefit of valuable baseball experience over the past 15 years, I am no longer comfortable that there is meaningful opportunity to continue my improvement at a satisfactory pace.
>
> As a result, after considerable thought and with sadness and disappointment, I have decided to end my baseball career.

sprints] if they don't have to," said Bulls reserve forward Larry Krystkowiak. "It was then I knew he was coming back." [74]

On Saturday, March 18, 1995, the speculation ended. If observers thought Jordan's statement on leaving baseball was terse, his statement on returning to the Bulls was even shorter. It arrived in media offices by fax messages sent by Michael's agent, David Falk. It read simply: "I'm back." [75]

Companies with which Jordan had endorsement contracts were almost as happy as Jordan, the Bulls, and the NBA. In the three days that followed his announcement, the stock value of five of those companies shot up by $2.3 billion dollars.

"Don't Give Up on Me Yet"

Jordan returned to action on Sunday, March 19, 1995, at Indi-anapolis's Market Square Arena. He was nervous about his return, and unsure of himself because his father was no longer there to give him advice. "He was my biggest adviser," Michael admitted, "and I had a tough time trying to move forward with-out him." [76] Jordan had trouble getting off the Bulls plane at the Indianapolis airport. He asked to stay behind. For an hour he sat alone, thinking of his father, and crying.

The rest of the world didn't know about the anguish Michael Jordan was facing. To them it was another media event. Tremendous excitement surrounded that first game, which

Although his father was no longer there to encourage him, Jordan received the support of enthusiastic fans who welcomed him back to basketball.

became the most watched regular-season NBA game in television history. "The Beatles and Elvis are back," exclaimed Indiana Pacers head coach Larry Brown. "It's a significant day."[77]

But Jordan wasn't really back. He was rusty. In that first game he wasn't Elvis *or* the Beatles. He was just 7-for-28, scoring a sub-par 19 points. The Bulls lost in overtime 103-96. Nobody—not even Jordan himself—knew for sure how rusty he really was—and whether it would ever wear off. In his first few games his shooting was off. He wasn't the Jordan of old. In the old days, when his teammates passed off to him, they were confident he could make the shot. Now, when they passed to him, it was almost as if they were trying to help his game. And there was the question of how he would fit in with his teammates on a personal level—after he had abandoned them and the game of basketball.

Jordan was rusty during the first few games he played with the Bulls. By his fifth game, Jordan was back in form.

Some people thought his coming back was as big a mistake as his having left in the first place. Former teammate John Paxson (now a Bulls announcer) called the whole situation "grotesque."[78] Jordan himself was a little nervous, sometimes sounding a little defensive about his talents. But deep down he knew he hadn't lost his skills. "Don't give up on me yet," he told one reporter.[79]

Jordan was right. In his fifth game back he stunned the New York Knicks by scoring 55 points. The Bulls needed all of those points as they barely squeaked by New York 113-111. Michael shot .411 and averaged 26.9 points, 6.9 rebounds, and 5.3 assists per game for the season. They were hardly "Jordanesque" figures, but they helped the Bulls to compile a 13-4 record over that span (and an overall 47-35 regular season mark) and to reach the NBA Playoffs.

Now it was the postseason—and surely Michael would shine once again. In the first game of the Eastern Conference Playoffs, he was the Jordan of old, scoring 48 points (18-for-32) with 9 rebounds and 8 assists as the Bulls downed the Charlotte Hornets 108-100 in overtime. That was as close as the Hornets came to the Bulls, as Chicago swept the series in four straight contests, winning the remaining games 106-89, 103-80, and 85-84. Jordan shot .495 and averaged 32.3 ppg. Maybe he *really* was "back."

The next stop was against the Eastern Conference champions, the Orlando Magic. Michael posted 31 points, 6.5 rebounds, and 3.7 assists per contest, but Chicago lost to Orlando in six games. Jordan seemed to have regained his scoring skills, but part of his touch was still missing. In the ten Playoff games he had committed 41 turnovers. "Number 23, he could just blow it right by you," said Orlando guard/forward Nick Anderson. "Number 45, he revs up, but he doesn't take off."[80]

Back to the Top

On October 2, 1995, the Bulls added a key component as they struggled to once again become the NBA's most powerful team. To the already strong combination of Jordan and Pippen they added eccentric six-foot, eight-inch forward Dennis Rodman. Rodman had started in the NBA with the "bad boy" Detroit Pistons of the 1980s. Traded to the San Antonio Spurs in 1993, Rodman continued to be the league's best rebounder, but his strange habits irked teammates and Spurs management. The heavily tattooed Rodman took to dyeing his hair a variety of strange colors— blond, green, red, blue, and even purple. "Our favorite: lime-jello green," noted Zander Hollander's *1996 Complete Handbook of Pro Basketball.* "It makes his head look like a Chia Pet."[81] Rodman also annoyed teammates by showing up late for practice. Despite his tremendous talent, the Spurs soon tired of Rodman and traded him to the Bulls for seven-foot center Will Perdue.

Bulls fans weren't quite sure what to expect from the very strange, and often very hostile, Rodman. What they got was his fifth straight rebounding title (14.9 per game) and an incredible season. The Bulls charged out of the box, winning 41 of their first 44 games. Before the regular season was over they had set an NBA record with 72 regular-season victories. With their overwhelming 72-10 mark, they became the first team in league history to reach the 70-victory mark. Michael Jordan? He had

Flamboyant forward Dennis Rodman joined the Bulls in 1995.

something to do with it, too, leading the NBA in scoring for the eighth time, with 30.4 points per game, and earning his fourth NBA MVP Award.

Jordan and Rodman had very different public images, but they got along fairly well—far better than Michael Jordan would have expected. Jordan explained:

> I can't say that I truly know him well enough to be his friend. He's my teammate. But people who say that he and I don't have conversations are wrong. We have lots of conversations, and they're very friendly. Frankly, they're more about basketball than anything else, because that's the one area of common ground we share.[82]

The Bulls swept the Miami Heat in the first round of the Playoffs, then went on to knock off the Knicks in just five games (and it took overtime for New York to win in game three). Then it was on to play against the tough Seattle Supersonics. It looked like Chicago would sweep Seattle, as the Bulls won the first three Finals games by scores of 107-90, 92-88, and 108-86. But suddenly Seattle sprang back to life, winning the next two games by scores of 107-86 and 89-78. In game six, however, the Bulls finally finished off the Supersonics, winning by an 87-75 margin.

In each game Jordan led the Bulls in scoring and won his fourth Finals MVP Award. After the last game he broke down and wept. Some might have thought that this was just another world championship for Jordan. But it wasn't. He had come back. He had proven the critics wrong. He wasn't finished, wasn't sliding downhill. He could still do it. He was still Michael Jordan.

Two-Peat

Much speculation swirled about the Bulls in the offseason. Jordan, Rodman, and coach Phil Jackson had all completed their contracts and could walk away from the Bulls for greener pastures. Jordan wanted to make sure both Rodman and Jackson signed with the team before he would commit himself. When they did (one year each—Rodman for $9 million and Jackson for $2.5 million), Jordan's agent David Falk began talks with Bulls

Dennis Rodman, Scottie Pippen, Phil Jackson, and Michael Jordan sit behind their NBA championship trophies. The Bulls had racked up an impressive four titles in six years.

owner Jerry Reinsdorf. When the talking was over, Jordan had engineered a one-year $30.14 million pact, the highest single-season salary in team sports history.

Yet, despite this returning talent—and despite the record 72 wins the Bulls had posted the year before—there was no guarantee that the team would repeat again in 1996–97. The team was not only getting richer—it was getting older, the oldest team in the entire NBA. Rodman would be 36; Jordan and backup center Bill Wennington, 34; guard Ron Harper, 33; Scottie Pippen and guard Steve Kerr, 31. The Bull's lone offseason pickup, seven-foot center Robert Parish, was even older at 43.

Yet Jordan retained an air of optimism about the upcoming campaign. "It should be a fun season," said Jordan, as the Bulls approached the 1996–97 season. "I anticipate us coming out and playing just as hard. We may not win 73 games or 72 games, but the ultimate goal is to win a championship." [83]

The Bulls didn't win 72 games in 1996–97—they only won 69, even though both Rodman (with a sprained ligament in his left knee) and Wennington (with a ruptured tendon in his left foot) ended the regular season on the disabled list. A lot of the credit had to go to Jordan, who again led the league with 2,431 points and 29.7 ppg.

Michael hoped he would win his fifth NBA MVP award, but that wasn't to be the case. In an extremely close vote (the second closest since reporters began voting on the honor in 1981), six-foot, nine-inch Utah Jazz forward Karl Malone defeated Jordan. Malone had finished second in scoring with 27.4 ppg.

Jordan also seemed overshadowed on his own team. Dennis Rodman led with 16.1 rebounds per game, but continued his controversial ways. In January he kicked a courtside cameraman. NBA commissioner David Stern fined Rodman $25,000 and suspended him for eleven games. The suspension cost him a lot more than the fine. Rodman lost over $1 million in salary during his banishment —and then had to donate the salary for his next eleven games to charity. And if that weren't enough, the California-based Carl's Jr. hamburger chain dropped the controversial Rodman from their advertising program. Between the multimillion-dollar signings, the never-ending focus on Michael, and Rodman's increasingly bizarre antics, the Bulls were turning into sports' favorite soap opera.

In the Playoffs the Bulls disposed of the Washington Bullets, Atlanta Hawks, and Miami Heat. Now came the real excitement, the NBA Finals—and Karl Malone, six-foot, one-inch guard John Stockton, and the Utah Jazz. Jordan wouldn't admit that he had a score to settle against Malone who had beaten him out of a fifth MVP Award. But it had to be on his mind.

Jordan was Jordan in game one, icing the contest with a twenty-one-foot jump shot right at the buzzer. In game two he scored 38 points in the Bulls' crushing 97-85 victory. But it was Utah's turn in games three and four, and they rallied to tie the series. Game five was at Salt Lake City's Delta Center, and it looked like the Jazz might take the series lead. The Jazz had won twenty-three road games in a row, and Michael was fighting a serious virus. He spent most of the day in bed, and Scottie Pippen said he had never seen his teammate sicker. Still fighting fever and dehydration, Michael took the court and made the Jazz feel sick, scoring 38 points (on 13-for-27) and hitting the winning three-point shot in Chicago's 90-88 win.

Back in Chicago, the Jazz led for most of game six, but Michael and the Bulls didn't want to be bothered by a game seven. They wanted to wrap it up that night. In the last quarter they poured it on, outscoring Utah 26-16. With just seven seconds left on the clock and two seconds left on the shot clock, the score was tied. Jordan had the ball. Everyone in Chicago's United Center expected he would shoot. The Jazz were determined Jordan would not beat them again—as he had in game one. John Stockton double-teamed him, cutting off his path to the basket. Jordan, however, had other plans. In the huddle he had told Steve Kerr, "Be ready." [84] Three men guarded Jordan, but Kerr was all alone, just a foot behind the foul line. Jordan surprised everyone by passing to Kerr. Kerr drilled a seventeen-foot jump shot to put Chicago ahead 88-86 as the shot clock hit zero.

Five-Time Champions

Utah still had time to tie things up—or even to go ahead on a three-pointer. Instead Tony Kukoc deflected Utah forward Bryon Russell's cross-court inbounds pass. The ball rolled loose. Scottie Pippen recovered it and passed to Kukoc. Kukoc dunked the ball. The Bulls were ahead 90-86—and it was all over. The Bulls were NBA Champions for the fifth time in seven years. Next to the fabulous Boston Celtics—the Chicago Bulls were now the second greatest dynasty in NBA history.

Michael had scored 39 points in game six, but that wasn't important. Winning was. "I'm so happy for Steve," Jordan said. "I'm glad he made that shot, because if he missed it he wouldn't have been able to sleep all summer." [85] But Jor-

Jordan and the Bulls defeated the Utah Jazz in six games, garnering a fifth NBA championship in 1997. The victory also gave Jordan his fifth Playoffs MVP award.

dan still won his fifth Playoffs MVP award. "I'll take the trophy," Jordan remarked, "but I'm going to give Scottie the car. He deserves it as much as I did."[86]

Staying Together

Following the Playoffs Jordan showed little sign of slowing down. A week and a half after the Playoffs ended, he signed a ten-year contract with CBS SportsLine. Jordan agreed to answer questions on the Internet, conduct monthly interviews, and act as a SportsLine spokesperson. Jordan would receive CBS SportsLine stock and a share of the company's ad and merchandise income that could eventually add up to $10 million.

In September 1997 Michael Jordan announced a new clothing line, the Jordan Brand, launched in cooperation with Nike. It would feature both clothing and footwear. Even though he was cashing in on his image, Jordan seemed upset that a number of newer athletes were moving too quickly into the product line:

> The brand exemplifies the way I try to be on the basketball court. Your personality determines your marketability. My personality has come out in the way I play and that's what has been marketed. Today, it's the opposite. A lot of players get marketed before they have that credibility.[87]

Meanwhile Jordan still had not signed with the Bulls. As in the year before, his first priority was to keep the winning Bulls combination together. Rumors were flying that Scottie Pippen (with whom Michael had grown increasingly close) was about to be traded. Jordan made sure everyone knew he'd be unhappy about that—and the trade never happened. Next he wanted Phil Jackson re-signed. Jackson got a new one-year contract—and a big raise—to $6 million. Only then did Michael sit down with Bulls owner Jerry Reinsdorf. When the meeting was over Jordan walked away with a bigger contract than ever—a one-year deal for $36 million.

Three-Peat—Part II

The Bulls had started the 1997–98 season looking strangely un-Bullish. Scottie Pippen was sidelined following foot surgery. The team began slowly, losing its first seven games. That sluggish start left them with only a 60-20 regular season record—good enough to make the Playoffs but not good enough to earn them home court advantage. Michael, however, was his usual self. He started each of the Bulls' 82 games, led the NBA with 28.7 ppg (his tenth scoring title), and captured his fifth NBA MVP award. On November 30, 1997, he even reached the 25,000-point plateau.

In the postseason Jordan averaged 36.3 ppg as the Bulls moved past the New Jersey Nets in three games. In the five games it took to beat the Charlotte Hornets he averaged 29.6 ppg. In the Eastern Conference Finals, it took a full seven games for Chicago to subdue coach Larry Bird's Indianpolis Pacers. Michael averaged 31.7 ppg, including a 41-point performance in game two.

In the Finals, it was a rematch of the Bulls against the Utah Jazz. Usually, when two teams met in the Finals two years in a row, the loser in the first year emerged victorious. The Bulls would have to work extra hard against Karl Malone, John Stockton, Jeff Hornacek, and the rest of the Jazz to overcome that jinx.

Adding to the Bulls' problems was their poor field goal shooting as the Finals continued. In game four they shot just 37 percent; in game five they made just 38.7 percent of their field goal attempts. In game five Michael was just 9-for-26, but he was far better than Scottie Pippen, who was a horrible 2-for-16.

To make up for their poor shooting the Bulls—and Jordan—redoubled their defensive efforts. "I knew the Bulls were a great defensive team," said ESPN analyst Dr. Jack Ramsey, "but they've exceeded my expectations."[88]

After four games the Bulls led three games to one, including a record 42-point blowout in game three. But Chicago couldn't end it all. In game five Karl Malone pumped in 39 points and the Jazz beat the Bulls 83-81. It looked like the momentum in the series was shifting back to Utah.

Game six was a nip-and-tuck battle—despite the 45 points Jordan would eventually score. It was in the final 37 seconds, however, that Michael would really shine. Utah held an 86-83 lead. Jordan got the ball and drove down court, blazing past Byron "The Man" Russell, for a layup. Now there were just 32.2

seconds left—and Karl Malone had the ball. Jordan sneaked up from behind and stole it away from the six-foot, nine-inch Utah forward. He moved toward the basket, faked out Russell and launched a jump shot from 17 feet out. Final score: Chicago 87, Utah 86. The Bulls had their sixth world championship (in just eight years) and their *second* "three-peat."

Once again there was talk about his retirement. "Hopefully I've put enough memories out there," said Jordan after the game. I have another life, and I know I have to get to it at some point in time. Hopefully the fans can understand that."[89]

After achieving his fifth championship title, Michael Jordan was ready to tackle the next season of play.

They might understand, but they would always want *more* Michael Jordan. He had more than established himself not only as the NBA's biggest star. He had become the greatest basketball player in history and the biggest sports star in decades. He was also a cultural phenomenon, an advertising phenomenon. He was a person who appealed to people regardless of his—or their—race.

He was bigger than labels (even designer labels), bigger even than his accomplishments. He was simply "Michael Jordan."

Notes

Introduction: His Air-ness

1. Quoted in Tom Weir, "'Goodbye to the Game': Michael Jordan, One of a Kind, Retires; Life Out of the Spotlight Is New Goal," *USA Today,* October 7, 1993.
2. Quoted in Alex Sachare, ed., *The Official NBA Basketball Encyclopedia.* 2nd ed. New York: Villard, 1994, p. 127.
3. Quoted in James Beckett, ed., *Beckett Great Sports Heroes: Michael Jordan.* New York: House of Collectibles, 1995, p. 77.
4. Nelson George, *Elevating the Game: Black Men and Basketball.* New York: HarperCollins, 1992, p. 234.

Chapter 1: Growing Up in North Carolina

5. Quoted in Gene Martin, *Michael Jordan: Gentleman Superstar.* Greensboro, NC: Tudor Publishers, 1987, p. 11.
6. Quoted in Jack Clary, *Michael Jordan.* New York: Smithmark, 1995, p. 19.
7. Quoted in Sally B. Donnelly, "Michael Jordan Can't Actually Fly, but the Way He Gyrates and Orbits on a Basketball Court, Driven by Fierce Competitiveness, It Sure Looks That Way," *Time,* January 9, 1989.
8. Quoted in Bob Greene, *Hang Time: Days and Dreams with Michael Jordan.* New York: St. Martin's Paperbacks, 1993, p. 44.
9. Quoted in Matt Christopher, *On the Court with . . . Michael Jordan.* Boston: Little, Brown, 1996, p. 12.
10. Quoted in Clary, *Michael Jordan,* p. 13.
11. Quoted in A. J. Carr, "UNC Tops Jayhawks in Opener," *Raleigh News and Observer,* November 28, 1981.
12. Quoted in Carr, "UNC Tops Jayhawks in Opener."

13. Quoted in Bill Gutman, *Michael Jordan.* New York: Pocket Books, 1995, p. 43.
14. Quoted in Beckett, *Beckett Great Sports Heroes: Michael Jordan,* p. 88.

Chapter 2: A One-Man Team

15. Quoted in Bob Logan, "Jordan Joins Youth Movement," *Chicago Tribune,* June 20, 1984.
16. Quoted in Donnelly, "Michael Jordan Can't Actually Fly."
17. Quoted in Clary, *Michael Jordan,* p. 44.
18. Quoted in Clary, *Michael Jordan,* p. 44.
19. Quoted in Bob Sakamoto, "A Bullish Beginning for MJ," *Chicago Tribune,* October 27, 1984.
20. Quoted in Bob Sakamoto, "In the End, Jordan's No. 1," *Chicago Tribune,* March 17, 1985.
21. Greene, *Hang Time,* p. 180.
22. Quoted in Greene, *Hang Time,* p. 127.
23. Quoted in Mitchell Krugel, *Jordan: The Man, His Words, His Life.* New York: St. Martin's Press, 1994, p. 151

Chapter 3: A Championship for Chicago

24. Quoted in Sam Smith, *The Jordan Rules.* New York: Pocket Books, p. 85.
25. Quoted in Smith, *The Jordan Rules,* p. 108.
26. Quoted in Smith, *The Jordan Rules,* p. 316.
27. Quoted in Beckett, *Beckett Great Sports Heroes: Michael Jordan,* p. 35.
28. Quoted in Melissa Isaacson, "Bulls Shoot for Three: It's Good!" *Chicago Tribune,* June 21, 1993.
29. Quoted in Beckett, *Beckett Great Sports Heroes: Michael Jordan,* p. 35.
30. Quoted in Jerry Bonkowski, "Bulls Air Their Feelings, Criticize Jordan," *USA Today,* October 4, 1991.
31. Quoted in Krugel, *Jordan,* p. 151.
32. Michael Jordan, *I Can't Accept Not Trying: Michael Jordan on the Pursuit of Excellence.* New York: HarperSanFrancisco, 1994, p. 22.

Chapter 4: Three-Peat

33. Quoted in David DuPree, "Dream Team Proving to Be a Nightmare to Opponents," *USA Today*, July 6, 1992.
34. Quoted in David DuPree, "Road to Olympic Gold Medal Held Little in Way of Suspense," *USA Today*, August 13, 1992.
35. Quoted in Skip Myslenski, "Jordan, Dream Team Have Golden Glow," *Chicago Tribune*, August 9, 1992.
36. Quoted in David DuPree, "Taking a Stand—in Reebok," *USA Today*, August 10, 1992.
37. Quoted in Sam Smith, *Second Coming: The Strange Odyssey of Michael Jordan—from Courtside to Home Plate and Back Again*. New York: HarperCollins, 1995, p. xxi.
38. Quoted in Smith, *The Jordan Rules*, p. xiii.
39. Quoted in David DuPree, "League-Best Bulls Eye NBA Title," *USA Today*, March 19, 1991.
40. Quoted in David Pietrusza, *The Phoenix Suns*. Springfield, NJ: Enslow Publishers, 1997, p. 31.
41. Quoted in David DuPree, "Jordan Drives at 55 / Bulls Push Suns to Brink," *USA Today*, June 17, 1993.
42. Quoted in David DuPree, "Jordan Rises to Challenge of Criticism," *USA Today*, June 18, 1993.
43. Quoted in Steve Ballard, "Bulls Savor Wins as Suns Commiserate," *USA Today*, June 22, 1993.

Chapter 5: "The Desire Just Isn't There"

44. Quoted in David DuPree, "Jordan's a Star Leaving in His Prime," *USA Today*, October 6, 1993.
45. Quoted in Greene, *Hang Time*, p. 210.
46. Quoted in Jack McCallum, "'The Desire Isn't There,'" *Sports Illustrated*, October 18, 1993.
47. Quoted in Krugel, *Jordan*, pp. 182–183.
48. Quoted in Rachel Shuster, "Jordan's Star Dims Only Slightly," *USA Today*, April 2, 1992.
49. Quoted in Krugel, *Jordan*, p. 206.
50. Quoted in Smith, *The Jordan Rules*, p. xiii.
51. Quoted in Smith, *The Jordan Rules*, pp. xiii-xiv.
52. Quoted in Jerry Kirshenbaum, "High Stakes," *Sports Illustrated*, June 14, 1993.

53. Smith, *Second Coming*, p. xv.

54. Quoted in Smith, *Second Coming*, p. 186.

55. Quoted in McCallum, "'The Desire Isn't There,'" 1993.

Chapter 6: A League of His Own

56. Quoted in Mike Dodd, "Associates Doubt He'll Come Back," *USA Today*, October 7, 1993.

57. Quoted in Mike Dodd, "Jordan, Jackson, Selleck Steal Spotlight at Workout," *USA Today*, July 13, 1993.

58. Quoted in Smith, *The Jordan Rules*, p. xi.

59. Quoted in Smith, *Second Coming*, p. 19.

60. Quoted in Smith, *Second Coming*, p. 21.

61. Quoted in Bob Greene, *Rebound: The Odyssey of Michael Jordan*. New York: Viking, p. 17.

62. Quoted in Murray Chase, "Jordan Signs Baseball Pact," *Albany Times-Union*, February 8, 1994.

63. Quoted in Steve Wulf, "Err Jordan," *Sports Illustrated*, March 14, 1994.

64. Greene, *Rebound*, p. 55.

65. Quoted in Bob Greene, "Of Shrieks and Question Marks," *Chicago Tribune*, March 6, 1994.

66. Quoted in David Pietrusza, *Minor Miracles: The Legend and Lure of Minor League Baseball*. South Bend, IN: Diamond Communications, p. 214.

67. Quoted in Pietrusza, *Minor Miracles*, pp. 214–215.

68. Quoted in Jim Patton, *Rookie: When Michael Jordan Came to the Minor Leagues*. Reading, MA: Addison Wesley, p. 146.

69. Quoted in Patton, *Rookie*, p. 219.

70. Quoted in Associated Press, February 12, 1994.

71. Quoted in Bob Greene, "Sox GM Forced His Hand: 'I Had to Get Out of There,'" *Chicago Tribune*, October 9, 1995.

72. Quoted in Greene, "Sox GM Forced His Hand: 'I Had to Get Out of There.'"

73. Quoted in Beckett, *Beckett Great Sports Heroes: Michael Jordan*, p. 114.

Chapter 7: "I'm Back"

74. Quoted in Smith, *Second Coming*, pp. 85–86.

75. Quoted in Greene, *Rebound*, p. 158.

76. Quoted in Smith, *Second Coming*, p. 1.

77. Quoted in Beckett, *Beckett Great Sports Heroes: Michael Jordan*, p. 23.

78. Quoted in Greene, *Rebound*, p. 165.

79. Quoted in Greene, *Rebound*, p. 167.

80. Quoted in Smith, *Second Coming*, p. 239.

81. Zander Hollander, ed., *The 1996 Complete Handbook of Pro Basketball*. New York: Signet, 1995, p. 291.

82. Quoted in Bob Greene, "Jordan on Rodman, Pippen, Jackson and Having Fun," *Chicago Tribune*, March 19, 1996.

83. Quoted in D. Orlando Ledbetter, "Bulls Know It Won't Be as Easy this Time Around," *Milwaukee Journal Sentinel*, November 1, 1996.

84. Quoted in Michael Wilbon, "Jordan Propels Bulls To 5th Title in 7 Years: Superstar Scores 39 Points to Sink Utah," *Washington Post*, June 14, 1997.

85. Quoted in John Jackson, "Thumbs Up! Bulls Win Fifth NBA Title," *Chicago Sun-Times*, June 14, 1997.

86. Quoted in Jackson, "Thumbs Up! Bulls Win Fifth NBA Title."

87. Quoted in Fred Kerber, "Jordan Fashions Killer Instinct," *New York Post*, September 10, 1997.

88. Quoted in Jeff Ryan, "Champs Again: Utah Made the NBA Finals Interesting, But It Couldn't Stop Michael Jordan and the Bulls When it Counted," *Sporting News*, June 24, 1998.

89. Quoted in Phil Taylor, "Six Shooter: Saving His Best For What May Not Be His Last, the Magnificent Michael Jordan Cooly Broke Utah's Heart and Led the Bulls to Another Title," *Sports Illustrated*, June 22, 1998.

Michael Jordan's Statistics

Regular NBA Season

YEAR	G	GS	MPG	FG%	3P%	FT%	RPG	APG	STL	BLK	PPG
1984–85	82	82	38.3	.51.5	.173	.845	6.5	5.9	196	69	28.2
1985–86	18	7	25.1	.457	.167	.840	3.6	2.9	37	21	22.7
1986–87	82	82	40.0	.482	.182	.857	5.2	4.6	236	125	37.1
1987–88	82	82	40.4	.535	.132	.841	5.5	5.9	259	131	35.0
1988–89	81	81	40.2	.538	.276	.850	8.0	8.0	234	65	32.5
1989–90	82	82	39.0	.526	.376	.848	6.9	6.3	227	54	33.6
1990–91	82	82	37.0	.539	.312	.851	6.0	5.5	223	83	31.5
1991–92	80	80	38.8	.519	.270	.832	6.4	6.1	182	75	30.1
1992–93	78	78	39.3	.495	.352	.837	6.7	5.5	221	61	32.6
1993–94						DID NOT PLAY					
1994–95	17	17	39.3	.411	.500	.801	6.9	5.3	30	13	26.9
1995–96	82	82	37.7	.495	.427	.834	6.6	4.3	180	42	30.4
1996–97	82	82	37.9	.486	.374	.833	5.9	4.3	140	44	29.6
1997–98	82	82	38.8	.465	.238	.784	5.8	3.5	141	45	28.7
TOTAL	930	919	38.6	.505	.332	.838	6.3	5.4	2306	828	31.5

NBA Playoffs

YEAR	G	GS	MPG	FG%	3P%	FT%	RPG	APG	STL	BLK	PPG
1984–85	4	4	43	.436	.125	.828	5.8	8.5	11	4	29.3
1985–86	3	3	45	.505	1.000	.872	6.3	5.7	7	4	43.7
1986–87	3	3	43	.417	.400	.897	7.0	6.0	6	7	35.7
1987–88	10	10	43	.531	.333	.869	7.1	4.7	24	11	36.3
1988–89	17	17	42	.510	.286	.799	7.0	7.6	42	13	34.8
1989–90	16	16	42	.514	.320	.836	7.2	6.8	45	14	36.7
1990–91	17	17	41	.524	.385	.845	6.4	8.4	40	23	31.1
1991–92	22	22	42	.499	.386	.857	6.2	5.8	44	16	34.5
1992–93	19	19	41	.475	.389	.805	6.7	6.0	39	17	35.1
1993–94						DID NOT PLAY					
1994–95	10	10	42	.484	.367	.810	6.5	4.5	23	14	31.5
1995–96	18	18	41	.459	.403	.818	4.9	4.1	33	6	30.7
1996–97	19	19	42	.456	.194	.831	7.9	4.9	30	17	31.1
1997–98	21	21	42	.462	.302	.812	5.1	3.5	32	21	32.4
TOTAL	179	179	41.8	.487	.332	.838	6.4	5.7	376	158	33.4

Legend: Basketball Abbreviations
G: Games Played
GS: Games Started
MPG: Minutes Per Game Played
FG%: Percentage of Field Goal Attempts Made
3P%: Percentage of Three-Point Attempts Made
FT: Free Throws
RPG: Rebounds Per Game
APG: Assists Per Game
STL: Steals
BLK: Blocked Shots
PPG: Points Per Game

Minor League Baseball Stats

YEAR	TEAM	LG	G	AB	R	H	2B	3B	HR	RBI	SB	CS	BA
1994	Birmingham	SL	127	436	46	88	17	1	3	51	30	18	.202
1994	Scottsdale	AFL	35	121	23	31	4	1	0	8	5	4	.256
	TOTAL		162	557	69	119	21	1	3	59	35	22	.214

Legend: Baseball Abbreviations
LG: League
G: Games Played
AB: At Bats
R: Runs Scored
H: Hits
2B: Doubles
3B: Triples
HR: Home Runs
RBI: Runs Batted In
SB: Stolen Bases
CS: Caught Stealing
BA: Batting Average

Important Dates in the Life of Michael Jordan

1963
Michael Jordan is born February 17 in Brooklyn, New York.
1970
Moves to Wilmington, North Carolina.
1980
Attends Howie Garfinkel's Five Star camp; named camp MVP.
1981
Graduates from Laney High School in Wilmington, North Carolina; finishes second in voting for North Carolina High School Player of the Year.
1984
Named College Player of the Year by the *Sporting News;* Drafted by Chicago Bulls, third overall in NBA Draft; Co-captain on U.S. Olympic Team; leads team to gold medal; Signs $2.5 million endorsement contract with Nike for Air Jordan.
1985
Chosen NBA Rookie of the Year; Breaks bone in foot, misses most of 1985–86 season.
1986
Scores record 131 points in three game Playoff Series; Scores single Playoff game record 61 points.
1987
Scores a record 23 consecutive points.
1988
NBA MVP and Defensive Player of the Year; NBA All-Star Game MVP; Jordan's first son, Jeffrey Michael, born in December to girlfriend Juanita Vanoy.

1989

Jordan marries Juanita Vanoy in Las Vegas on September 2; Phil Jackson becomes Bulls head coach.

1990

Scores career-high 69 points in a single game; Jordan's second son, Marcus James, born in December.

1991

NBA MVP; Playoff MVP; NBA Finals MVP; leads Bulls to first NBA title; Hosts "Saturday Night Live".

1992

NBA MVP; Playoff MVP; NBA Finals MVP; leads Bulls to second NBA title; Plays on U.S. Olympic Team; leads team to gold medal.

1993

Playoff MVP; NBA Finals MVP; leads Bulls to "Three-peat" third straight NBA title; sets NBA finals record with 241 points; opens Michael Jordan's Restaurant in Chicago; Jordan's father, James Jordan, is murdered in Lumberton, North Carolina in July; Jordan announces his retirement in October.

1994

Plays minor league baseball with the Birmingham Barons and the Scottsdale Scorpions.

1995

Announces return to NBA on March 18; plays first game on March 19; Dennis Rodman joins the Bulls.

1996

NBA MVP; NBA All-Star Game MVP; NBA Finals MVP 1996; Selected as one of the 50 Greatest Players in NBA History; leads Bulls to fourth NBA title.

1997

NBA Finals MVP; leads Bulls to fifth NBA title; Re-signs with Chicago Bulls; Introduces Jordan Brand of apparel; breaks Kareem Abdul-Jabar's record for consecutive games with at least 10 points—his 788th game in that record; reaches 25,000-point plateau.

1998

NBA MVP; NBA Finals MVP; leads Bulls to sixth NBA title.

For Further Reading

Nathan Aaseng, *Sports Great Michael Jordan.* Springfield, NJ: Enslow, 1996. A short biography of Jordan.

Peter C. Bjarkman, *Sports Great Scottie Pippen.* Springfield, NJ: Enslow, 1996. A very brief biography of Jordan's teammate, Scottie Pippen.

Matt Christopher, *On the Court with . . . Michael Jordan.* Boston: Little, Brown, 1996. A popular biography of Jordan.

Jack Clary, *Michael Jordan.* New York: Smithmark, 1995. An illustrated biography by a veteran sportswriter.

Gene Garber, *Hoops!: Highlights, History, and Stars.* New York: Friedman/Fairfax Publishers, 1994. A well-illustrated history of the NBA.

Chip Lovitt, *Michael Jordan.* New York: Scholastic, 1993. Not as well-known as Matt Christopher's biography of Jordan, but perhaps better.

Gene Martin, *Michael Jordan: Gentleman Superstar.* Greensboro, NC: Tudor Publishers, 1987. A biography written fairly early in Jordan's career.

Ken Shouler, *The Experts Pick Basketball's Best 50 Players in the Last 50 Years.* White Plains, NY: All Sports Books, 1997. A look at Michael Jordan and other basketball greats. Not surprisingly Jordan rates number one.

Works Consulted

Books

James Beckett, ed., *Beckett Great Sports Heroes: Michael Jordan.* New York: House of Collectibles, 1995. This book about Jordan is from the producer of several memorabilia magazines and includes material on Jordan memorabilia as well as on his career.

Peter C. Bjarkman, *The Encyclopedia of Pro Basketball Team Histories.* New York: Carroll & Graf, 1994. Dr. Bjarkman's history of the NBA divides the subject team by team and includes a chapter on the Bulls.

Chuck Daly with Alex Sachare, *America's Dream Team: The Quest for Olympic Gold.* Atlanta: Turner Publishing, Inc. 1992. Coach Daly tells what it was like to take the Dream Team to Olympic Gold.

Lori Flores, ed., *Chicago Bulls 1996–1997 Media Guide.* Chicago: Chicago Bulls, 1996. An extremely well-produced and elegant guide to the Bulls issued by the team for the media.

Nelson George, *Elevating the Game: Black Men and Basketball.* New York: HarperCollins, 1992. A look at how African-Americans have changed basketball.

Bob Greene, *Hang Time: Days and Dreams with Michael Jordan.* New York: St. Martin's Paperbacks, 1993. This best-seller paints a sympathetic portrait of Jordan.

———, *Rebound: The Odyssey of Michael Jordan.* New York: Viking, 1995. Greene chronicles Jordan's return to the NBA after his brief baseball career.

Bill Gutman, *Michael Jordan.* New York: Pocket Books, 1995. A well-done biography of Jordan for younger readers.

Zander Holander, ed., *The 1996 Complete Handbook of Basketball.* New York: Signet, 1995. A guide to the 1996 NBA season.

Michael Jordan, *I Can't Accept Not Trying: Michael Jordan on the Pursuit of Excellence.* New York: HarperSanFrancisco, 1994. A brief insprirational book by Jordan.

Mitchell Krugel, *Jordan: The Man, His Words, His Life.* New York: St. Martin's Press, 1994. A biography with a heavy emphasis on Jordan's own words.

Jim Patton, *Rookie: When Michael Jordan Came to the Minor Leagues.* Reading, MA: Addison Wesley, 1995. An account of Jordan's short-lived baseball career that oozes hostility. You can see why Jordan shied away from some reporters.

David Pietrusza, *Minor Miracles: The Legend and Lure of Minor League Baseball.* South Bend, IN: Diamond Communications, 1995. Contains a short section on Jordan at Birmingham.

———, *The Phoenix Suns.* Springfield, NJ: Enslow Publishers, 1997. A brief history of the NBA's Phoenix franchise, written for younger readers.

Alex Sachare, ed., *The Official NBA Encyclopedia.* 2nd ed. New York: Villard, 1994. A very useful guide to the history of the NBA and its players' records.

Sam Smith, *The Jordan Rules.* New York: Pocket Books, 1994. This book critiques Jordan's reputation as a flawless superman.

———, *Second Coming: The Strange Odyssey of Michael Jordan—from Courtside to Home Plate and Back Again.* New York: Harper-Collins, 1995. Smith examines Jordan's return to the Bulls.

Martin Taragano, *Basketball Biographies.* Jefferson, NC: McFarland, 1991. This book provides brief biographies of 434 players, coaches, and contributors to the game of basketball.

Rick Telander, *In the Year of the Bull: Zen, Air, and the Pursuit of Sacred and Profane Hoops.* New York: Simon & Schuster,

1996. A look at the Bulls' 1995–1996 season, with an emphasis on Jordan, Dennis Rodman, and coach Phil Jackson.

Periodicals

Associated Press, February 12, 1994.

Steve Ballard, "Bulls Savor Win as Suns Commiserate," *USA Today,* June 22, 1993.

Jerry Bonkowski, "Bulls Air Their Feelings, Criticize Jordan," *USA Today,* October 4, 1991.

A.J. Carr, "UNC Tops Jayhawks in Opener," *Raleigh News and Observer,* November 28, 1981.

Murray Chase, "Jordan Signs Baseball Pact," *Albany Times-Union,* February 8, 1994.

Mike Dodd, "Associates Doubt He'll Come Back," *USA Today,* October 7, 1993.

———, "Jordan, Jackson, Selleck Steal Spotlight at Workout," *USA Today,* July 13, 1993.

Sally B. Donnelly, "Michael Jordan Can't Actually Fly, but the Way He Gyrates and Orbits on a Basketball Court, Driven by Fierce Competitiveness, It Sure Looks That Way," *Time,* January 9, 1989.

David DuPree, "Dream Team Proving to Be a Nightmare to Opponents," *USA Today,* July 6, 1992.

———, "Jordan Drives at 55 / Bulls Push Suns to Brink," *USA Today,* June 17, 1993.

———, "Jordan Rises to Challenge of Criticism," *USA Today,* June 18, 1993.

———, "Jordan's a Star Leaving in His Prime," *USA Today,* October 6, 1993.

———, "League-Best Bulls Eye NBA Title," *USA Today,* March 19, 1991.

———, "Road to Olympic Gold Medal Held Little in Way of Suspense," *USA Today,* August 13, 1992.

———, "Taking a Stand—in Reebok," *USA Today,* August 10, 1992.

Bob Greene, "Jordan on Rodman, Pippen, Jackson and Having Fun," *Chicago Tribune,* March 19, 1996.

————, "Of Shrieks and Question Marks," *Chicago Tribune*, March 6, 1994.

————, "Sox GM Forced His Hand: 'I Had to Get Out of There,'" *Chicago Tribune*, October 9, 1995.

Melissa Isaacson, "Bulls Shoot for Three: It's Good!" *Chicago Tribune*, June 21, 1993.

John Jackson, "Thumbs Up! Bulls Win Fifth NBA Title," *Chicago Sun-Times*, June 14, 1997.

Fred Kerber, "Jordan Fashions Killer Instinct," *New York Post*, September 10, 1997.

Jerry Kirshenbaum, "High Stakes," *Sports Illustrated*, June 14, 1993.

D. Orlando Ledbetter, "Bulls Know It Won't Be as Easy this Time Around," *Milwaukee Journal Sentinel*, November 1, 1996.

Bob Logan, "Jordan Joins Youth Movement," *Chicago Tribune*, June 20, 1984.

Jackie MacMullan, "Break Up the Bulls?: Owner Jerry Reinsdorf Says He May Do It—Win or Lose," *Sports Illustrated*, May 5, 1997.

Peter May, "Entitled: After Defeating The Jazz in Six to Win The Championship, The Bulls Deserve to Stay Together and Play for One More Ring," *Sporting News*, June 23, 1997.

Jack McCallum, "'The Desire Isn't There,'" *Sports Illustrated*, October 18, 1993.

————, "Friends and Foes Together," *Sports Illustrated*, May 31, 1993.

————, "The Lips Were Zipped," *Sports Illustrated*, June 7, 1993.

————, "They're History," *Sports Illustrated*, June 28, 1993.

————, "Triple Play," *Sports Illustrated*, June 21, 1993.

————, "Who's Running the Bulls?" *Sports Illustrated*, February 15, 1993.

Skip Myslenski, "Jordan, Dream Team Have Golden Glow," *Chicago Tribune*, August 9, 1992.

Shaun Powell, "Jordan Takes Center Stage: As Usual, His Airness Is Leading the Bulls to the Title," *Sporting News,* June 6, 1997.

Rick Reilly, "Smells Like Another Rose," *Sports Illustrated,* June 21, 1993.

Jeff Ryan, "Champs Again: Utah Made the NBA Finals Interesting, But It Couldn't Stop Michael Jordan and the Bulls When it Counted," *Sporting News,* June 24, 1996.

Bob Sakamoto, "A Bullish Beginning for MJ," *Chicago Tribune,* October 27, 1984.

———, "In the End, Jordan's No. 1," *Chicago Tribune,* March 17, 1985.

Rachel Shuster, "Jordan's Star Dims Only Slightly," *USA Today,* April 2, 1992.

Sam Smith, "MJ Will Be Back with Bulls—and Even Richer," *Chicago Tribune,* June 3, 1997.

Phil Taylor, "Six Shooter: Saving His Best For What May Not Be His Last, the Magnificent Michael Jordan Cooly Broke Utah's Heart and Led the Bulls to Another Title," *Sports Illustrated,* June 22, 1998.

Tom Weir, "'Goodbye to the Game:' Michael Jordan, One of a Kind, Retires; Life Out of the Spotlight Is New Goal," *USA Today,* October 7, 1993.

Michael Wilbon, "Jordan Propels Bulls To 5th Title in 7 Years: Superstar Scores 39 Points to Sink Utah," *Washington Post,* June 14, 1997.

———, "Jordan Tries to Stop Ruining of the Bulls," *Washington Post,* June 15, 1997.

Steve Wulf, "Err Jordan," *Sports Illustrated,* March 14, 1994.

Index

Picture Credits

Cover photo: Allsport USA
Agence France Presse/Corbis-Bettmann, 91
Allsport USA, 7, 8, 11, 14, 16, 19, 22, 28, 39, 40, 42, 49, 54, 55, 69, 73, 81, 82, 84, 88
AP/Wide World Photos, Inc., 27, 34, 35, 50, 60, 64, 67, 71, 77, 86
Corbis-Bettmann, 25 (bottom)
Reuters/Corbis-Bettmann, 45, 51, 65 (both)
UPI/Corbis-Bettmann, 18, 25 (top), 44, 62

About the Author

David Pietrusza's works for young readers include *The End of the Cold War, The Invasion of Normandy, The Battle of Waterloo, John F. Kennedy, The Chinese Cultural Revolution, Smoking,* and *The Roaring Twenties,* all published by Lucent Books.

Pietrusza has also written extensively on the subject of sports. He served as President of the Society for American Baseball Research (SABR) from 1993 through 1997 and is co-editor of *Total Baseball,* the official encyclopedia of Major League Baseball, and managing editor of *Total Football,* the official encyclopedia of the NFL. Pietrusza is also the co-editor of the books *The Total Baseball Catalog, Total Braves, Total Indians, Total Mets, Total 49ers, Total Steelers, Total Packers,* and *Total Cowboys.* He has written five books on baseball (*Judge and Jury: The Life and Times of Judge Kenesaw Mountain Landis, Lights On!, Minor Miracles, Major Leagues,* and *Baseball's Canadian-American League*), three works on baseball for young readers (*Top 10 Baseball Managers, The New York Yankees,* and *The Los Angeles Dodgers*) and two works for young readers on basketball (*The Phoenix Suns* and *The Boston Celtics*). In 1994 Pietrusza served as a consultant for PBS's Learning Link on-line system and wrote and produced the documentary *Local Heroes* for PBS affiliate WMHT.

He lives with his wife, Patricia, in Scotia, New York.

4 - 2|o| | 2|.o|